For my late mother

CONTENTS

FOREWORD

The word *sustainability* not too long ago was always associated with corporate social responsibility (CSR), which tends to focus on philanthropic and social matters. The concept of CSR has since been expanded to cover the triple bottom line, management of business profits, people, and the environment.

When I was in the oil-and-gas industry, sustainability was part and parcel of the business. It was embedded in the work practices, systems, processes, and mindset of people involved in the industry. The extractive nature of the industry and consequence of mal-operations which could be catastrophic ensured that all involved understand not only the health and safety issues but also the sustainability of the business.

Today, sustainability is almost a buzzword which has a much larger meaning and coverage. Nothing in business could be conducted without the consideration of sustainability, be it environmental, economic, social, or financial. Organisations and institutions ranging from legislators, corporations, civil societies, and individuals are all aware of the need and implication of sustainability.

The subject of sustainability reached its pinnacle when nations came together to adopt the Sustainable Development Goals (SDG) initiated by the United Nations in 2015. From thereon especially, governments all over the world introduced policies, laws, and regulations in support of the SDG aimed for a better world for its inhabitants. Businesses also started to extend the triple-bottom-line approach to cover areas under the SDG. New technologies and innovative approaches were introduced to support the goals.

However, the impact of sustainability or applying sustainability is still a challenge especially for small and medium industries and individuals. Individuals being consumers have a major role to play, as they could exercise their rights to subscribe or otherwise to businesses that put sustainability on their business agenda. They could also make a difference by applying sustainability in their daily lives. Small and medium industries, which constitute the bulk of industries in many countries, have a major role to play in sustaining sustainability.

This book, *Applying Sustainability*, is timely as it provides not only an overview of the subject of principles and practices of sustainability in the areas covered, but more important is the practicality (i.e. the how) on how sustainability can be applied. The book covers and describes issues also relating to sustainability as a subject make its implications and how we address them accordingly. Sustainability can be a dry subject, but the author has turned it into something that is basic and understandable. All relevant topics are covered, ranging from issues on education, gender, resources, consumption, investment, including Industrial Revolution (IR) 4.0 that is embraced by the world.

It is hoped also that this book will spark interest and be good reference material for anyone who wishes to understand the subject of sustainability and the applied aspect of sustainability.

Going forward, business as usual is no longer acceptable. New and innovative approaches are required to ensure no waste and no emissions are generated. The aim at the end of the day is to achieve social, economic, and environmental prosperity for all and make this world a better place for everyone.

Datuk Ir. (Dr) Abdul Rahim Hj. Hashim
Vice Chancellor
University of Malaya

ACKNOWLEDGEMENTS

I acknowledge my deep appreciation to Felicity Healey-Benson for her comments on initial drafts, but equally significant is her personal contribution of the chapters 'Sustainability and education' and 'Humans versus Robots'.

INTRODUCTION

There are already hundreds of books written about sustainability. There are many interpretations used interchangeably over its concepts, principles, and philosophy.

Sustainability in business is essential in today's hyperconnected world, where information is readily available or transmitted within seconds. Businesses that embrace transparency, responsibility, and discipline have a better chance of sustaining success, so says the study of companies in *Good to Great* by Jim Collins.

The world we know has changed so much. Many in both advanced and emerging markets grew up with the conveniences of modern living, with the necessities of electricity, water, and transportation taken for granted. While material consumption has risen steadily, the overconsumption of raw materials and the resultant wastes are often ignored.

All these developments have unintended consequences on the earth's diminishing resources. Excessive carbon emissions into the earth's atmosphere have been blamed for climate warming with detrimental effects on food security, nutrition, and water supply.

More recently, the excitement over the fourth industrial revolution has drawn critical attention to the future of industries driven by data management, automation of processes, and the introduction of robots. These bring a new set of sustainability challenges.

Addressing these complex sustainability challenges must be interdisciplinary and multidisciplinary, drawing upon the relevance and application of economics, environment, and society. Indeed, the transformation of corporate and societal attitudes is required. Such a shift in mindset is necessary for the world community to realise a more sustainable future.

Sustainability cannot be addressed independently. Its application and contextual understanding must be integrated to ensure its outcomes are achieved with maximum impact. As businesses embrace their sustainability strategy, they will need to transgress the necessary principles of sustainability, adopting a more holistic approach.

Concept

The broad concept and application of sustainability principles vary across issues and diverse stakeholders. Sustainability leadership demands the principles of transparency, commitment, innovation, and inclusiveness be applied across all aspects of its application and delivery.

It is not surprising that for the business community to better understand the acceptance of sustainability language in business mainstream, the process demands a higher business commitment towards the environment and its social obligations, beyond that of compliance to rules and reputation management.

The triple-bottom-line concept of profits, environment, and people has become acceptable business language especially among the multinationals. Business sustainability, also known as corporate sustainability, is therefore the management of environmental, social, and economic demands through application of its principles to ensure responsible and ethically acceptable practices across all domains of economy and society.

Principles

Sustainability principles and leadership applied at strategic level require a statement of intent, key directions, and commitment towards embracing the greater transparency and stakeholder inclusiveness.

There are already many corporations with sound and robust sustainability strategy. Such evidence of changing corporate attitudes is not only meeting performance expectations of their stakeholders, but evidently, there is recognition that such good practice brings tangible benefits, especially enhanced corporate image and reputation. This can be seen also in their increased reporting on the impacts of sustainability endeavours. The development of integrated reporting has helped to assure public of their commitment towards corporate responsibility. There has been an increase in the awareness of the environmental impact or possible risks of business processes.

Businesses and corporations today are better informed of their environmental responsibility, going beyond obligations towards recycling and waste management. Enter the concept of circular economy. It is not new, but increasingly relevant in today's context.

All of these have enabled businesses to redefine and rebuild their supply chain management, including the introduction of responsible sourcing, and there are increasing numbers that have embraced circular practices including recycling and reusing of material for their production. Sustainable businesses are expected to realign their operational processes from development, production to services. For some, bold investments in the appropriate technology to produce or harness renewable energy will help support sustainable goals, but many may be put off by the high initial cost of investment. The use of renewable energy to drive the business economies has seen mixed outcomes. Many, however, will face the challenge of increased costs, where the business case for acquiring new technology may be costly and they may find applying sustainability principles may not be favourable.

Yet it will take some years before it complements or replaces the more traditional business model of linear production, where use-and-discard behaviour would have adverse environmental issues.

In today's digital age, where information is accessed at the touch of a finger, businesses and increasingly organisations are concerned over what employees think of them at present and in the future. Workplace engagement, including health and safety today, is now a minimum obligation, with increasing relevance for employers to expand upon their social responsibility. This includes community development and their stand on global issues, including human trafficking, climate change, gender inequality, international trade, use of plastic, etc.

The need to improve social sustainability performance has become important to not only businesses, but also a wider range of stakeholders. Gains made in employee engagement, community relations, philanthropic activities, or health and safety are easily quantified. Doing good business at both international and local level is now equally important. Goals include the organisational contribution towards making communities safer and healthier places to live, especially so for resource and extracting industries.

Global corporations have a world audience. They are obliged to demonstrate best practice in social responsibility. This requires a higher standard of governance and responsibility ensuring minimum expectations on standards in human rights, hiring, and community management. A significant element of this governance responsibility is the opportunity for companies to build and strengthen their stakeholder engagement, including building proper risk-mitigating plans. A poorly executed social sustainability plan can backfire if proper measures on health and safety and hiring policies are below the minimum legal standards.

Market engagement continues to evolve with consumers becoming more discerning and better informed. The Internet age has enabled consumers to be aware of the products they purchase, and importantly the opinions of others. Consumers are sensitive to the value of brand performance they tend to be familiar or associated with, and the environment standing of the company is a key criterion.

Within this context, businesses are expected to use their influence to propagate their values and commitments towards environment protection, including recycling, use of organic products, doing no harm to animals, etc. Integration of these sustainability actions reflects the expected changes to the way companies decide, and their relationship with local stakeholders. While there are risks that must be managed, equally there are challenges and opportunities to fall in line with the global stand on sustainability.

Application

Applying sustainability principles and practices requires more than a statement of intent. How this is done has to start with clarity on how business defines its own concept of sustainability, its practicality, relevance, and measures. There are great examples of companies that have succeeded in not only embracing the principles but also acquiring and sustaining the standards that continue to develop over time. These examples are, however, far and few between.

Equally there are those who have used sustainability as a public relations exercise, making use of the 'giving back to society' concept, which is often a one-off charity exercise or a donation to a nearby school project.

One of the key success factors of sustainability is commitment. This refines the way a business model is shaped and delivered. Business responsibility towards sustainable business practices has begun to gain more traction. Potentially this is because many big businesses have found a sustainability strategy to support business advantage, including an enhancement in brand value, efficiency, environment stewardship, and community relations.

In a broader context, social, environmental, and profit demands are the three pillars of sustainability. It is now well understood that the *triple bottom line* concept is a gradual departure from the more traditional bottom-line management.

Strategic goals

This book, *Applying Sustainability*, is organised around the broad strategic themes of sustainability and its *principles and practices*. The book acknowledges the complexity over the sustainability issues and debates over the implementation challenges.

The book contains twenty-eight chapters, each written to give the readers a better understanding of the challenges, concerns, and the outcomes so far in the range of solutions applied in both principles and practice, internationally and nationally.

From a business and social perspective, *Applying Sustainability* revisits the debate on the definition of sustainability ethics and asks whether such principles can be taught and legislated for.

Applying Sustainability reminds readers of the United Nations' SDGs adopted in September 2015 by all its member states. The essays written in the book consider issues on education, gender, resources, consumption, investment, housing all in the context of these global goals. The intent is giving a better perspective of the challenges and issues as well to gain a view of *where we are* now in relation to the outcome target for the year 2030.

Applying the sustainability actions to support the SDGs is never going to be easy. To begin with, the concept and relevance between businesses vary. There is a perception that the larger corporations, being more visible, have taken sustainability initiatives more seriously. For others, especially those in small- and medium-sized industries, the acceptance and understanding of the importance of sustainability are seen to be slow but increasing.

On a global front, the agenda of embracing the culture and practice of sustainable development is increasingly taken more seriously by both governments and businesses. Since the first Earth Summit back in 1992, the agenda for SDGs has since been accepted by all member countries in 2015, which outlines a clear vision for sustainability that protects the environment and society and will not compromise the needs of the future generations.

The SDGs define the actions to be taken, and the measures to ensure it does not compromise its standards. Issues from gender inequality to resource deprivation to climate change and its implications are urgent areas where each member state has been asked to do something.

Applying Sustainability includes more recent external impacts on sustainable business. In the next decade, technology disruption to traditional jobs, services, and education is likely to continue. It is within such a context Felicity Healey-Benson's chapter on 'Human versus Robots' addresses the fresh implications on technology sustainability. A recurring theme, the impact of technological change on sustainable development involves the displacement of humans by robots but requires the advancement of science to sustain humankind. Digital technology is well acknowledged and positioned to help achieve the SDGs not only in conservation of precious resources, but it includes a culture of recycling and reuse in resource management. A key facilitator in the achievement of a non-dystopian future, however, is the continuing investment in human skills and a transformative education system.

Technology advancement in mobile application and cloud technologies has also been applied across markets including the emerging circular economies. In poorer parts of the world, the solar grid has been installed and applied to provide safe and affordable energy for lighting and cooking, instead of the traditional use of the polluting firewood or kerosene.

Measures

The book pays attention not only to resources utilisation, highlighting the cost of plastic waste and the recycling of material disposal, but also to doing good for environment and society. The circular economy and its contribution to sustainability are also reviewed.

It would be fair to suggest that sound sustainability can best be described as one that combines all ethical business, environmental, and community responsibilities. But it is necessary that all three elements are brought together into a new holistic business approach, where sustainability becomes a natural approach.

By addressing the issues on a wide range of important sustainability topics, the book hopes to promote that sustainability is not just about doing charity or every greening or environmental activity but more about sustainability's principles.

The added value of sustainability is measurable these days, with more businesses pursuing environmental and social change. One can hope for incremental changes in the future, especially in helping to reach a more sustainable future, but will this be enough in time?

Applying business sustainability principles which promote responsible business and behaviours will require stakeholders not only to embrace moral change but also to pursue different practices where such changes can be made easier with technology and artificial intelligence. It is expected that technology will contribute to a more sustainable future for the planet and future generations, but such debate isn't so straightforward, as technology can also speed up the destruction of the very resources one hopes to protect.

The development of a non-financial measurement for sustainability has already advanced, with integrated reporting accepted as a new benchmark of measures. Understandably, the challenges of applied sustainability will not go away overnight, but it is important to get the balance right in a real world. The balance means ensuring there is an equilibrium between qualitative and quantitative objectives and outcomes, i.e. economically sound and efficient with an acceptable level of responsibility in environment and ethical and social behaviours towards diverse stakeholders and communities.

Future

On this note, *Applying Sustainability* advocates change not only in business model, but also in the way businesses, governments, individuals, multinational agencies accept and integrate sustainability principles and governance for respective opportunities. New perspectives can complement the traditional model, but new opinions and rethinking on management of resources are necessary in order to navigate a difficult world. Climate change, for example, cannot be seen in isolation but also is a business risk to investments and access to resources. Concerns on diminishing resources and waste cannot be left to high-level policy debate alone; conservation management must be taught, to build both capacity to change and capability to manage. Business implications of climate change are real, and it makes sense for business to integrate such risk into its strategy. There are also opportunities in re-charting the sustainability future which considers the best use of robotics, artificial intelligence, and new applications of digital technology.

There is no shortage of solutions to meet future needs, but nothing less than what sustainability stands for matters.

CHAPTER 1

Can ethics be taught?

Applying sustainability principles demands inclusion of a wider set of stakeholders. It calls for ethical and responsible behaviours. Ethical sustainability calls for stakeholders to uphold the moral standards and ethics. These demands will always face challenges especially in situations where individuals or businesses may be required to accommodate certain standards of behaviour that they may find inconvenient or unfamiliar.

But if the global communities are serious over the idea of applying sustainability principles to their business and society mainstream, then the case for adoption of sustainability practice and principles will need to be strengthened, simplified, and sustained in both depth and breadth.

Decades of economic progress and developments have led to rapid depletion of precious resources including diminishing forests and resources on land and sea, like fresh water. The linear production that has been so successful in producing goods and services to satisfy the growing appetite of its population, but the end product of its consumption is waste that needs to be got rid of.

Societal dependence on fossil fuels that have powered industry and services is another example. But the release of greenhouse gas that comes from use of these fossil fuels, primarily coal and oil, is now being regarded as the primary cause of climate change. The unintended consequence poses the ethical dilemma for all stakeholders.

The issues of social sustainability are many. But one of the concerns involves the widening of the income inequality between the rich and poor. Addressing this takes efforts and time. But sustainable living demands a more functional system where access and means will constantly need to be addressed.

Numerous cases of corporate failures in modern times, from Enron almost two decades ago to bank failures not too long ago, questioned the moral system that includes values, ethics, and behaviours. Business historians are quick to deduce that poor moral standards and ethics are to be blamed rather than poor regulation.

Within the financial services industry, which has more than its fair share of unethical scandals, the root cause of such unacceptable behaviours—for example, pursuit of self-interest and greed—is to do with values, environment, and behaviours, among the many reasons often cited. This reflects the possible failure of the traditional moral standards and ethical principles, both of which are pillars to sustainable living. Such ethical misdeeds have caused much damage financially to the wider stakeholders, but it is equally important to point out that public interest has been compromised. It reinforces the authorities' conviction that a major overhaul and installation of the industry ethos and professionalism as the main engine of the industry are an urgent must-do on the agenda. Hence, there are enough justifications for an education in ethical sustainability, where ethics becomes the core of the curriculum and an integral part of the learning outcome.

Ethics agenda

A quick browse in the Google search engine for ethical scandals will not only result in more 125 million hits, but the topic is universal across diverse cultures and industries. A point which has often been debated and has attracted much attention is whether ethics in business can be taught.

Today in a complex world with much uncertainty and volatility, leading business schools are the first to defend their curriculum to counter the argument that business schools are churning out graduates who have no concern for unethical behaviours and practices. One of the learning objectives of MBA courses is to ensure business school graduates are equipped with the knowledge and understanding of the right values and behaviours in their future roles. No business school can take this for granted.

Learning

The debate over whether ethics can be taught has been going on over the past two decades. No one has the complete answer, but the debate has left behind more questions than answers. But many professors will agree that ethics classes will not convert every student into a more ethical citizen, but the professors at Stanford Business School in one of their events themed 'Does teaching ethics do any good?' agree that they do teach their MBA students to engage more confidently in ethical dialogues.

Business schools have included an ethics module as one of the electives or even a core topic in the postgraduate qualifications. The learning approach varies from understanding meaning of values and behaviours to one at Arizona State University, where students are being requested to take an oath as 'evidence' of their commitment to be ethical leaders. There are others who do not insist but open their minds to the bigger picture of what it takes to be an ethical leader, and repercussions if they don't.

One common approach among leading business schools includes helping students to understand the concepts of ethical business and values, and these are being deployed to handle the related issues in the courses. It is not uncommon to find business schools that use case-study approach allowing students to understand and apply the principles and concepts of ethics and professionalism. There will always be the challenge of selecting the appropriate balance for such value-based education. Differing culture practices and acceptance are one. But an acceptance of universal standard within the context of sustainability principles will be relevant.

The rationale for such an approach is the opportunity to test real-life examples where different perspectives and opinions are being debated. Interestingly, values and cultures do play a part in producing contrasting viewpoints. It is interesting to note that ethical guiding principles can derived from religious beliefs, and these are important for teaching ethical sustainability.

While the use of case studies allows critical thinking, it gives students a better understanding to relate and explain ethical issues and complexities. In many cases today, the ability to relate and exemplify the understanding of ethics in business and society does give students the edge in job hunting and future careers.

Education on ethical sustainability and principles should also be part of the lifelong learning across all jobs and responsibilities. The application of ethical knowledge and skills, for example, will always question the balance between the social and environment objectives and the business needs. The sustainability agenda will always include the question of the moral judgement of doing good.

Reforms on training curriculum have already taken place to ensure ethical competence be included and applied, focusing on the behaviours of integrity and application of moral value across industry practices. Ethics training needs to be delivered through a series of applied case studies, proper testing, and reinforcement at various stages of learning—formal and informal. Beyond the teaching and learning environment, ethics in its standards and forms is also reinforced through institutions and processes.

Institutions and processes

In the United Kingdom, the financial services industry with the help of regulators established the Banking Standards Board (BSB), whose remit is to promote a high standard of behaviour and competence across UK banks and building societies. The BSB worked with their member banks and others, including consumer bodies, professional bodies, universities, to identify how best to increase and improve the ethical standards of behaviour and competence in banking. Among the deliverables rolled out are

1. Consumer framework to identify the good banking practices and outcomes
2. Guiding principles on raising standards of professionalism
3. Education, learning, and research work including exposure to real-life case studies.

BSB has a strong advocacy role for higher standards of ethics, responsibility, and professionalism across the local financial services industry. Recognising the contagion risk from its observations of the inherent interconnected nature of global banking, it has a purpose to ensure the convergence and harmonisation of standards of professionalism and ethical behaviours through the sharing of research, international best practices, and partnership with the industry.

Regulators recognised that the local industries have no choice but to embrace and integrate the wider agenda of professional ethics from boardroom to shop floor, which includes ensuring the code of ethics is well understood across the business mainstream and reminding staff to fulfil continuing professional development (CPD) requirements like business and professional ethics.

Code of conduct

While research studies show that education and training may solve half the problem towards shaping and reinforcing the ethical culture, corporate cultures and leadership play a more crucial role towards shaping the employee behaviours, reinforcing the ethical values within the internal environment through introduction of a code of ethics as necessary support to ensure the promotion of right behaviours and values.

The introduction of the industry code of ethics to support the standards of professional conduct is to ensure members of the industry fraternity observe the expected standards to act or serve their stakeholders—including customers, peers, and business partners—with integrity, competence, diligence, and respect. This is in line with regulated professions such as accountancy; legal and medicine and bank professionals must always also act ethically to the public, clients, employers, colleagues, and others in the industry. Employees in the banks, for example, are also expected to complete successful the mandatory online assessments. To complete successful, individuals are expected to demonstrate the understanding and the application of the standards across compliances and money laundering, and risk management across the markets the institutions operate.

Another step many global banks have taken forward is the application of its of code of ethics. The code of ethics designed to support the standards of professional conduct typically defines specific behavioural requirements and commitment to professionalism, integrity, and discharging duties to clients, employers, and the institute. The purpose of the code is also to ensure clear benchmarks against which customers, colleagues, and others can measure their ethical and professional competence. By doing so, the public will be duly informed and assured by the commitment of the banking industry to practise a higher level of ethical professionalism.

A typical code of ethics sets out the following key attitudes and behaviours it expects of banking professionals.

1. Treating all customers, colleagues, and counterparties with respect and integrity;

2. Considering the risks and implications of my actions and advice, and holding myself accountable for them and for the impact these may have on others;

3. Complying with all current regulatory and legal requirements and following best industry practice;

4. Treating information with appropriate confidentiality and sensitivity;

5. Being alert to and managing potential conflicts of interest which may arise while performing my role;

6. Developing and maintaining my professional knowledge and skills; and

7. Acting always in a fair, honest, trustworthy, and diligent manner.

Such focus on standards of professionalism is intended to raise higher levels of public confidence and trust, as well as improve credibility among customers. For bankers for example, this is about sustaining a culture of professional development and continuous improvement, and pride in the profession.

Implicitly, the code is designed to ensure good standing of the professional body which the members come from and represent. The code is consistent with many other organisational and professional body codes. This will bring the financial services professionals in line with the high standards of professionalism expected of many professions where public interest is key.

They are expected to understand and agree to subscribe to the code and to embed its principles within their organisations. This is a must within the industry, such that behaviours are part of the mainstream—encouraged, recognised, and rewarded. It should not remain a 'do as you are told'; rather, such values must be woven into the organisational culture, or 'the way things are done here'.

Standards of professional conduct

The standards of professional conduct will not only demand a set of well-defined behavioural standards on professionalism and integrity; they are expected to comply with laws and regulations, and exercise independence and objectivity. In a regulated financial service sector, employees are prohibited from insider trading, tipping, and market manipulation. Employees must also exercise duties of fairness and objectivity and observe strictly client confidentiality.

Professional conduct includes rules on their duties in observing loyalty to their employers and avoidance of potential conflict of interest. Indeed, any potential conflicts of interest must be disclosed openly and fairly.

The standards of professional conduct will place special mention of confidentiality, conflict of interest, and honesty. The underlying guiding principles will include a more definitive list of explanations on client confidentiality, disclosures, investment decisions, and arresting potential conflicts. Ensuring clients' interests is an intended outcome of the professional code.

Beyond learning

In grappling with the issues of ethical concerns at workplace, many employers will face the challenge of not only putting in place a robust framework in an already regulated environment. Educating employees on the importance of ethics is part of the corporate sustainability, which corporations must embrace and be accountable to the interest of environment and community at large.

The code of ethics is not without its shortcomings. The very set of standards in values and practices will not be of help if these are ignored. But importantly, the presence of the code will not stop any organisation from continuing to use resources that are harmful to environment or use material (for example, plastic) that will become waste after use.

In this context, it is necessary for corporations and businesses to ensure public interests are protected through professional conduct and actions reflecting the values of responsibility and standards they espoused. Walking the values may make more sense to demonstrate its commitment and to fulfil public expectations of its corporate responsibility.

In the final analysis, the value propositions are clear—the responsibility of businesses and corporations in upholding ethics standards to protect the interest of the community at large is expected, and high ethical standards cannot be compromised. Ethics, in other words, can be taught but reinforced within the framework of monitoring and enforcement of institutional values and processes.

CHAPTER 2

Realising the UN Sustainable Development Goals (SDGs)

In 2015, the world leaders met to agree to the UN-led set of seventeen broad sustainable development goals for a better planet by 2030. These bold steps are aimed at three broad objectives:

1. eradicating poverty
2. addressing inequality
3. tackling climate change.

The United Nations' SDGs are uniquely placed to be inclusive, involving governments, businesses, civil society, and the public to work on a common agenda towards a sustainable future for future generations. The concept of sustainable development in this context covers a broad scope of areas, involving economic, environmental, and social aspects.

Each of the following sustainable development goals and targets serves as guidelines for each of the developments.

Goal 1: No Poverty
Goal 2: Zero Hunger
Goal 3: Good Health and Well-being
Goal 4: Quality Education
Goal 5: Gender Equality
Goal 6: Clean Water and Sanitation
Goal 7: Affordable and Clean Energy
Goal 8: Decent Work and Economic Growth
Goal 9: Industry, Innovation, and Infrastructure
Goal 10: Reduced Inequality
Goal 11: Sustainable Cities and Communities
Goal 12: Responsible Consumption and Production
Goal 13: Climate Action
Goal 14: Life Below Water
Goal 15: Life on Land
Goal 16: Peace and Justice Strong Institutions
Goal 17: Partnerships to Achieve the Goal
Source: United Nations

SD goals criticised

The UN-backed sustainable development goals do have their own set of sceptics, one of whom is Ruth Kattumuri of the Asia Research Centre at the London School Economics, who observed and criticised that the goals have not gone far enough, especially on social issues. She acknowledged that while much of the economic and environmental concerns and security were extensively covered, she was of the view that the seventeen goals did not address the depth of the each of the goals. For example, not much has been spoken of addressing human trafficking problems, where in dollar value the illegal trade is estimated to be worth more than $30 billion. It is an industry that exploits and violates the human rights of hundreds of thousands of men, women, and children each year and must be addressed worldwide.

There are others who have considered such sustainable goals to be too broad and lacking focus. Many had the view that sustainable goals would only make good guidelines and execution will be a challenge in the context of other economic and social priorities. In less-developed nations, governments are already battling against many social concerns, including rising incidence of poverty, youth unemployment, and widening wealth gaps between the rich and the poor.

Ongoing concerns

Globally, public complaints over the escalating increase in food prices are on the rise. Ironically, much of the increase can also be blamed on unpredictable but hostile climate conditions. For example, in 2018, prices of wheat grain skyrocketed because of prolonged drought in Russia and unexpected flooding in Pakistan. Such patterns are expected to be repeated, given the expected swing in the climate patterns. Disruption to the economics of food grains is to be expected each time supplies are affected by the least predictable changes to climate conditions. Any increase in the price of staple grains will certainly affect the cost of livestock feed, leading to eventual global increase in food prices, and hence put more pressure on the millions of people who live and work on small farms, especially in emerging countries.

Paradoxically, such a concern was one of the many issues that were expressed at the launch of *2018 New Climate Economy* on 12 September 2018, by the United Nations secretary general António Guterres, who warned member states that the full force of climate change is a real possibility. Precisely because of the consequences of the grave climate challenges, actions must be taken to prevent severe repercussions if no actions are taken in the next two years.

He backed up his strong words with examples of unpredictable extreme weather that are more frequent, violent and real threat to communities. There is a general agreement that the climate change has to do with the hurricane Florence that brought much damage and misery to the communities in the state of Carolina, United States. Similar extreme weather saw Japan recording its hottest summer in more than seventy years in 2018.

Report on the breaking up of ice shelf in West Antarctic is a concern. Scientists have predicted the break-up of the glaciers in the Antarctic would raise sea levels by a foot by year 2100. Already frequent reports of flooding in the most unexpected places and the prolonged outbreak of forest fires in Australia, California, Brazil, and southern Europe, for example, are evidence that has kept planners and environmental experts awake. Experts are naturally very worried and concerned that the lack of global leadership to address effectively such a sustainability concern will bring about even worse consequences for the global communities. But the worry is over the worsening environmental conditions, for example, intensity of climate changes that makes any adaptation plans redundant, hence an inevitable uncontrollable climate change.

Big picture

Taking a broader view, the SDG represent a sensible but inclusive blueprint to achieve a better and more sustainable future for all. These are the most comprehensive objectives produced of late, and rightly so, these UN-backed goals are aimed to address the global challenges we face, including those related to poverty, inequality, climate, environmental degradation, prosperity, and peace and justice. The SD goals are interconnected, and although the target is 2030, there are already many examples where these are being used as targets as part of respective national aspirations among the participating governments.

Beyond the basics

Addressing the sustainability agenda is not just about supporting a more inclusive and balanced economic growth. Decades of uninterrupted urbanisation and industrialisation have delivered increased living standards, but the amount of resources used increased twelvefold between 1900 and 2015. The World Economic Forum White Paper on Circular Economy reported that in the past forty years alone, global use of materials has tripled, from 26.7 billion tonnes in 1970 to 84.4 billion tonnes in 2015, and these figures are expected to rise with rising consumerism and affluence, especially in emerging economies.

Sustainable goals are far more than that; they provide a vision of sustainability that embraces the integration of economic, environmental, and social responsibilities. By considering a myriad of environmental and social aspects, there has been conscientious effort towards the efficient consumption of natural and social capital, as well managing the waste that is being produced. Examples are seen even in reuse of old building materials, harvesting of wastewater, and even the reuse of discarded IT equipment.

The achievement of all the SD goals will need to embrace the culture of sustainability that will require the changing of attitudes, habits, and mindsets towards management and ethical practices developing the right ethos and behaviour norms across work and society at large. Despite the improved awareness of better sustainable living, the WEF white paper recognised several barriers including transition cost, high investment costs, awareness, bureaucracy, resistance to change, consumer apathy; all these pose challenges.

Sustainability leadership

There is enough evidence that sustainability does matter if the SD goals are to be achieved. Sustainability leadership in governments requires each of them to be fully aware and to consider global trends, challenges, and changes. It is necessary to ensure its development strategies be designed to manage risks or to seize new opportunities for sustainability purposes.

In coping with the threats and risk, there are already nations deliberately planning a greener development involving new technologies to harness renewable energy, and by being efficient in energy consumption, they can account for greater savings and by being responsible, they can enhance the reputation of brands and products.

In business too, efforts are not spared in harnessing and maximising the resources which reduce carbon emission yet add greater competitiveness. One example is in the construction industry. In the past, little attention was given to the impact the construction and operation of buildings will have on the environment. Typically, the construction industry would consume high energy, timber, and water resources. But with the high cost of energy to light and cool buildings, it has made business sense for property management to innovate the application of design methods to reduce energy consumption and deploy renewable energy, such as solar, to be more efficient and sustainable.

The strategy to reduce carbon footprint as part of global sustainability targets was well articulated at the Paris climate agreement. While support and commitment from governments and large corporations towards setting and achieving the reduction in carbon emissions remain positive, there is still some way to go before energy efficiency and conservation efforts yield necessary results.

Managing waste

One of the consequences of rapid economic growth has been the increase in the amount of waste generated, from both production and consumption trends. Much of the amount of waste per capita (an average individual produces 2 kg per day) is a result of rapid population growth and improved lifestyle. The explosive growth of plastics for packaging, as an example, is a concern. Rising affluence brings an increase in consumerism, where people buy more than they need. It is difficult for example for people to change in lifestyle, and the lack of willingness among many companies to accept such responsibility continues to worsen the problem of waste management. Such changes in lifestyle have resulted in an increase in non-degradable plastics and papers used for wrapping and packaging. The process of recycling introduced to both industry and household has not made much difference (less than 5 per cent of all waste is recycled) as environment-friendly policies continue to be ignored by many and consumers are apathetic or ignorant towards the importance of a greener environment.

Nonetheless, public opinions are increasingly in favour of greater environmental responsibility, protection of heritage, and public health and safety. Demand for sustainability leadership therefore is urgent, as there are still complaints of industrial pollution or total disregard for environment care and health and safety issues.

Business and culture of sustainability

Sustainability as a strategic imperative has to be applied across various business supply chains, involving product packaging and safety, consumer rights, and governance and reporting compliances. Today, much of these are enabled by eco-friendly support and technology.

Importantly, the acceptance of a sustainability culture sponsored by their major stakeholders does make a difference to the operations. No longer can a business operates in isolation, without taking into consideration its implications and relationship with the wider society.

In the information age, individuals and corporations are being watched more carefully. Irresponsible behaviours— from accounting frauds and abuse of human rights to industrial accidents—are no longer tolerated, and such irresponsible acts can now be captured online within minutes. Non-governmental organisations and concerned citizens are now speaking up on public abuses and overdevelopment in their neighbourhood. Investors too are showing greater interest in socially responsible investments while insisting on acceptable but improved standards and transparency. Employees too want greater engagement with the corporate leaders that put ethical leadership and values at the forefront of the corporate agenda.

Achieving sustainable goals isn't a bad thing. It offers every stakeholder bright and inclusive challenges and opportunities to improve their lifestyle, and for businesses, it impacts on the way we engage, work, and interact. A sustainability agenda should be strategic—where organisations can identify how to overcome threats and take advantage of opportunities and the changes in a very volatile but unpredictable world to create a better future.

Values and public interests

In such a context, the SD goals should be viewed from business values and public interest. At work, businesses should align their employee commitment to SD goals, in order to gain employee commitment and trust. The new generation of employees is more informed, and they want more work–life balance. New job seekers will want to be associated with companies that embrace sustainability. The inclusiveness means a greater respect for different values and cultures and harnessing of their strengths has proven to be one of the success factors behind good to best companies. The sustainability challenges can no longer ignore public expectations and interest.

The varied and often conflicting demands from stakeholders will continue to rise, and therefore, it will make sense to establish a sustainability agenda that mirrors the UN sustainable development goals. To inculcate and walk these values requires all stakeholders to play their part so that a sustainable culture can be promoted. This comes with protecting public interest and responsibility at the heart of it all.

CHAPTER 3

Legislating responsibility

The definition of corporate social responsibility (CSR) refers to 'businesses going beyond their purpose to meet or exceed the ethical, legal, public expectations and commercial obligations'. The World Business Council for Sustainable Development (WBCSD) defines the term *corporate social responsibility* as '*the continuing commitment by business to behave ethically and contribute to economic development while improving the quality of life of the workforce and their families as well as of the local community and society at large*'.

The term CSR is often interpreted and understood differently, but in practice, each term is interpreted according to context, intent, and purpose. The concept of CSR has a long history associated with the impact of organisational behaviours on communities and society. Fast forward, CSR is now more commonly known to many as business responsibility for its influence and impact on society. The term is better understood in today's context; businesses are now expected to meet increased stakeholder expectations.

These stakeholders include not just shareholders but also employees, consumers, suppliers, and the community at large.

The concept of CSR has evolved over time. There are hundreds of debates over the use and meaning of each of these terms that have been used interchangeably and understood differently on occasions, notably *corporate responsibility*, corporate citizenship, and governance.

CSR to sustainability

Following the release of the report by the Brundtland Commission (formerly the World Commission on Environment and Development) in October 1987, the term *sustainable development* became more popular. The concept of sustainability was naturally integrated into the mainstream of business practices. Sustainability is now being treated as business concept to demonstrate its responsibility to diverse stakeholders and society. Sustainability is not a just a concept; it is about everything each business indulges, from compliance to responsible sourcing. Business strategies see this as one of the risk pillars as well as opportunities to engage in sustainable practices with diverse stakeholders.

Leading companies do build in sustainability strategy to demonstrate business accountability to society, involving both environmental and social responsibility. Already there are many such global firms committed to United Nations Sustainable Development Goals by partnering with external parties to address a number of long-term global issues on environmental pollution, global warming, climate change, water crisis, youth unemployment, poverty, and gender inequality.

Much of the growing business commitments towards global or issues are largely voluntary. This is because businesses regard this as part of their commitment to doing good business and an extension of their efforts in fostering a strong corporate governance culture and ensuring their responsibility to the interest of wider stakeholders and community they serve.

Much of these efforts are encouraging, especially so when businesses are still coming to grips with increasing need to comply beyond the minimum standards, including the need to embrace greater practices of corporate responsibility. The term *corporate responsibility*, over time, was preferred by businesses that wanted to place greater emphasis on the business side of their enterprise rather than social, which to many is narrow but has a philanthropic slant.

Today, the concept of corporate sustainability has gone wider because of additional requirements from regulators for companies to be more in line with the changes that aim to protect public interests and minority shareholders. It is now clear to those who would want to stick to the old-fashioned CSR concept, as they do it because of deliberate intent to give back to society through contribution to social cause, but this includes scholarships for education and funding charity activities.

It does not come as a surprise that the concepts of *CSR* or *corporate responsibility* or *corporate sustainability* are understood differently, although each has a different set of objectives and expected outcomes. From the external perspectives, all of these are regarded from the ethical perspective in business dealings. Whether the business becomes more socially responsible in its business practices or environmentally conscious or more generous with their social responsibility, many accept the voluntary nature of sustainability. There are those who want the practice to go beyond discretionary, arguing that making sustainability practices mandatory is the right moral thing to do.

Regulation so far

The justification to push business beyond their responsibility of focusing only on profit has been debated for a very long time. There are already a number of regulations in place to ensure more ethical practices to be embedded in industries. The financial services industry is a good example. There are also enough rules and regulations in most company acts to ensure companies comply with rules and law on environment, public services, and protection of consumers' rights and public interest. Employees' rights and benefits that include health, safety at the workplace, and social security are compulsory at advanced and emerging markets.

Governments increasingly require greater transparency from the bigger corporations to address a wide range of corporate responsibility issues and stakeholder demands in addition to the more traditional shareholder needs. In some markets, mandatory corporate responsibility reporting requirements focusing in particular on non-financial disclosure and activities have been put in place already. The non-financial disclosure requirements are overwhelmingly social activities and programmes including health, safety, and environment. Increasingly, the reporting criteria include internal governance of business, including remuneration decisions and environmental and social implications of business. Top-level management are more involved and engaged to take corporate sustainability beyond just mandatory reporting.

Against mandatory responsibility

There are good reasons why corporate responsibility policies and practices should not be made mandatory. Sustainability is not confined to just being a good corporate citizen; rather, it is about constantly innovating change to create a better future for both business and the communities it serves. Sustainability today is about helping diverse stakeholders to apply rational economic principles, respecting government regulations, including innovation breakthroughs to build a better world. Meeting the sustainability goals will require strategic orientation including stakeholder engagements and leaders who have the ability to see not only risks but also opportunities with partners and competent collaborators.

There is no doubt that the adoption of sustainability principles will gain strength over time, and business and corporations will do well to monitor the impact of the intangibles through better management of the sustainability intelligence and analytics as their business processes, including risk management and compliances.

Given the changing tide of globalisation, those who are able to adapt their sustainability strategy will find this to be a key differentiator in competing for the scarce commodities of human and financial capital. International financial capital, whether in the shape of foreign direct investment (FDI) or portfolio funds, is increasingly being scrutinised, as it too is subject to the demands from their own stakeholders to put responsibility at the top of their agenda. Beyond this, there are many examples of sustainability efforts that have taken place across the globe.

Engaging consumers

Today's consumers live in a digital environment with fast and greater access to information, and they are therefore better informed. Most surveys show consumers are receptive and sensitive to products that are not environment friendly, which explains why standards and labelling have been on the rise to ensure consumers are better informed.

Consumers are also employees. In a battle for talent, this is one possible consideration for employees to decide the employer they want. The seriousness with which companies adopt aspects of responsibility and sustainability is fast becoming a plus point or important reason behind job seekers' decision to accept employment.

Building skills

A recent report, Globalization Next Chapter, by McKinsey Global Institute shares the view that global companies are increasingly building local pools of skilled workers for the domestic supply chain, and this has significantly changed their approach towards human resource policies. In many ways, they are investing more sustainability principles in local supply chains.

Innovating

Indeed, the current challenges of geopolitics and threats of tariff wars have accelerated the trend towards rethink over future trade and investments. But in the areas of responsibility and sustainability issues, there have been developments and innovations. Examples of these include stakeholder management by PepsiCo and innovation by Nike. Coca-Cola, a USD8 billion company, has placed its priority on sustainability leadership, which will be its central focus to build a thriving business and communities. For example, the drinks company has invested much, including technology, to improve efficient use of plastic, water, and energy resources, all of which are part of sustainable development. Businesses elsewhere are innovating and inventing in new sustainable breakthroughs that will use technologies to build much more sustainable communities that are within the sustainable development goals.

Environment stewardship

Environment stewardship is a sustainability issue. Unwelcome reports of pollution, ecological degradation, employment of illegal workers, and hazardous waste are headlines for the wrong reasons. No longer can corporate leaders ignore the perils of pollution and its effect on local environment and community.

It is an acceptable fact that climatic change has become more acceptable as a risk and concern. There is also a problem with waste disposal. Even in a country with heavy rainfall, rivers are likely to be polluted, threatening the source of clean water for the public. Already there are laws against pollution, which require a more consistent enforcement and consumer education.

Social engagement

One of the significant changes local businesses can do is to develop and strengthen its social partnership with civil society organisations. Greater corporate citizenship engagements will include identifying key issues and putting in place initiatives that are beneficial to all parties. Issues that will generate interest include pollution, business ethics, biodiversity, ethical products, human rights, and supply chain management. Hence, they also provide business and corporations the corporate social opportunities to demonstrate their obligations to the society they operate in as well as avoiding any potential consumer protests, as demonstrated in the extraction and plantation industries.

Business case

It is very clear there is a stronger case for corporate responsibility to remain voluntary, which can create greater value benefitting the wider stakeholders. It is hard to see how a mandatory corporate responsibility can be any better, other than an increase in the allocation of corporate donations. It also means having businesses to shoulder the social cost of additional fiscal taxes or sponsorship a typical CSR event. The imposition of mandatory corporate responsibility activities will slow down innovations.

As Richard Welford, chairman of CSR Asia, said in his article in the CSR Asia weekly, governments do not understand the links between CSR and corporate brands, reputation, and trust. They cannot understand the business case for every single business because it will be different for each one.

CHAPTER 4

Addressing low income

Much has recently been said and written of low-income countries progressing from their status to become middle-income nations. The WEF even reported the total number of low-income countries has nearly halved to thirty-four, as some thirty-one have graduated to middle-income status. It is very evident in the WEF report that much of this success is attributed to the economic growth and success.

Low income

Despite acquiring the new income status, rising costs of living in a number of these middle-income nations have posed new challenges to the bottom 50 per cent of domestic households. It is very disturbing to know a high percentage of these households do not have savings. Those in bottom 40 per cent of household income are hardest hit, especially with recent rises in food prices. The World Bank studies show that there are easily two billion people in the world whose livelihood depends on food production; the irony is that while food prices continue to rise, the farmers do not necessarily benefit from such development.

The vulnerability of such risk further questions the sustainability of progress, which should be immediately addressed. The report on zero savings in half of the total households is very revealing but hardly surprising. It is even surprising to note that 20 per cent of domestic households are only able to survive less than three months should they lose their income and this in an environment where 65 per cent of the workforce are in paid employment.

Rising gap

One example is Malaysia which is officially classified as an upper middle-income country. The resource-rich country, however, faces the same problems of rising income inequality, and the bottom 50 per cent is getting no better. Despite its higher income status in terms of gross national income, which stands at almost US$13,000, the increasing cost of living has become a major concern among the locals from the bottom 40 per cent of households. It is acceptable as fact (including a report from the Khazanah Research Institute on the state of Malaysian households) that the main concerns among the poorer people centre on the rising cost of housing, education, healthcare, etc.

Citing reasons for such a disturbing trend, the report highlighted increased fuel prices, rising living cost made worse by a weak foreign exchange that have all imposed greater burden on the lower householders.

A survey conducted by the Debt Management and Counselling Agency (AKPK) reported that three out of ten working adults have had to borrow money to buy essential goods. This poses a massive risk to individuals, as it shows little or no capacity to save, and no safety net if they lose their capacity to earn.

The agency, in their report, pointed out the rising living costs are one reason why many do not even the capacity to save, let alone cope with the additional financial burden.

Such national concern has alerted the policymakers, and the non-governmental organisations are aware of such risk, which should be immediately addressed.

Little or no savings

One of the highlights in the report shows that half of the total households have zero savings. The report is a revelation, and it was even surprising to note that 20 per cent of domestic households are only able to survive less than three months should they lose their income, and this in an environment where 65 per cent of the workforce are in paid employment.

The economic environment is even more unpredictable with modest growth expected, but no one can predict whether the current employment can be sustained, and unemployment rate of 3.5 per cent controlled.

The outlook becomes even more risky when household debt reaches a high of 89.1 per cent of total earnings. While the Central Bank has assured the country in the past the ability to service debt remains sound, a high-debt economy may not be sustainable when the low-income groups are most affected by rising cost of living and threats of job losses.

Rising living costs

The rising costs of living are a common challenge facing many young families in middle-income nations. Many can no longer afford to buy homes, unlike their parents, and higher living standards also demand higher commitments. Many graduates are also in debt by the time they land their first jobs. It is no surprise that household debt in several developing nations has been rising.

Boosting the minimum wage in several middle-income markets has also helped to increase wages, and this has contributed to alleviation of urban poverty. In many instances where there are low-wage and hourly jobs and this increasingly must come with greater flexibility with the work schedules to balance erratic work hours with possible opportunities to earn their second income, and for working families, time for caring for their families. Ever-changing work schedules make all of these, including accessing childcare, important first steps to make sustainable lifestyles where balancing work and family is made possible.

Role of government

Economists would be quick to point out that creation of high-value jobs would be one of the ways to improve incomes. Even in the most advanced economies, politicians would place the creation of new jobs on their list of priorities. Governments are in the best position to do just that; through their access to resources, governments are in the best position to invest in job-creation activities such as rebuilding its physical infrastructure or using incentives through fiscal measures, growing new areas such as developing renewable energy sources or rejuvenating abandoned housing and revitalising urban areas and investments across various job-creation activities.

Governments are also in the position to provide macroeconomic policies to stimulate economy through a wide range of fiscal and monetary means, including joint ventures with foreign-based companies.

However, all said and done, many middle-income economies face the challenges of a new economic environment that is more unpredictable and volatile, with no expert able to predict whether the employment can be sustained, let alone contain rising unemployment among the youth. Many middle-income nations face the dilemma of discarding the low-cost strategy in favour of higher income, but it comes with possibly lower employment potentials and higher costs of investment.

Climate change

Another threat to lower-income groups comes from the consequences of climate change, including volatility in weather patterns that would impact on food production which the poor depend on, but also a long-term impact on the food prices. There is no doubt that low-income communities in both urban and rural areas will be disproportionately impacted by climate change; relative to others, the poor would take longer to recover. This is also the conclusion of the International Monetary Fund (IMF) in its world economic outlook as reported by the *Financial Times (FT)* of 17 October 2017. In short, the report concluded by saying the poor are innocent victims of changes for which they bear no responsibility.

While the IMF offered no simple solution, it did point out the responsibility of each government to manage the weather changes with mitigating solutions. Interestingly, as part of adaptation policies, *FT* suggested the deployment of relevant technologies, but more importantly, a moral case for rich nations to help with the challenges of climate change and its impact on the poor.

Economic solution

A longer-term sustainable solution is to raise incomes of the vulnerable households, but this comes with tangible increase in its productivity. Productivity, rightly so, has been recognised as an important contributor to the Malaysian government agenda on the fourth industrial revolution, which promotes innovation amid the period of disruptive technology and change. Put it simply, routine and so-called low-value work are slowly but surely being replaced by large-scale automation, outsourcing, and innovations, part of ambitious plans to step up productivity in the service sector. As the largest contributor to the country's GDP at 53.5 per cent, the service sector is the largest employer, with 8.6 million people. The sector includes financial services, auditing and accounting, outsourcing services, tourism, retail.

Re-skill

Having the right set of high-end skills is one agenda relevant stakeholders will have to push as a number one priority. Acquiring new skills must be part of this productivity agenda for it to succeed. This is of paramount important as employers gradually reduce their hiring for low-end jobs or even resort to outsourcing jobs that are routine, repetitive. Such trends as already experienced in the financial services industry have seen the rapid disappearance of clerical jobs over the years. The future of work is to go with the changes to the delivery channels of institutions such as banks, and jobs will simply require skills to interpret and advise as their roles go upstream.

Another example is based on a *FT report* that predicts trend in the future of roles in the audit business. This comes as a result of disruptions in the workflow automation, and introduction of artificial intelligence, which will shape the future of audit.

The challenge is ensuring employers do the right thing, which is to encourage and ensure their new skills are acquired, applied, and appreciated.

It is easier said than done. Encouraging the workforce to be reskilled will require not only persuasions but capacity support. Challenges include putting in place a work culture that nurtures, motivates, and encourages the right behaviours, including sincerity and learning. Leaders will need to do more than lip service, and they will need to be inclusive in their approach, and to recognise learning as one of their roles and responsibilities.

Digital learning

In today's digital era, choice of learning is simply made easier and accessible. Many courses, from languages to financial planning, are delivered online with study support and resources at affordable price. Indeed, self-certification with even classroom tutorials is available so readily to assist learners to gain accreditation for career progress or even to start their own businesses.

Indeed, workforce at all levels should be empowered to pick up new skills regularly if they want to stay relevant or serve the markets better. On average, poor families who pay out of pocket for education tend to spend a higher proportion of their disposable income. Furthermore, such affordability may be only confined to a few and not all.

Boosting investments in education will help more struggling families to obtain the means to higher income in order to improve their income and even mobility. On paper, rising productivity provides the opportunity for a substantial rise in the pay for those who have succeeded. The trickling-down effect can only take place when the pay policies are well designed to recognise the differences.

No one disagrees with the philosophy that with productivity gains comes the need to share prosperity through income growth. It is after all a sustainable development agenda of reducing inequality that with a high-income nation comes higher productive but better-paid workforce. Such goal is within the grasp of the government.

Challenges

The challenge is ensuring employers do the right thing, which is to encourage and ensure their new skills are acquired, applied, and appreciated.

It is probably easier said than done. The lack of accessible, affordable, high-quality working adult education serves as a major barrier to higher income status.

CHAPTER 5

Impact of climate change on nutrition

The Rome 2014 Declaration commits participating governments to eradicate malnutrition of all forms, by giving diverse communities at international, regional, national, and local levels access to nutritious diets through its policies and actions on food and nutrition sustainability.

Rome declaration

The declaration acknowledged the far-reaching impacts of climate change on food security. The commitment was agreed against the background of a warning among many scientists that the global temperature is set to rise above the minimum tolerance level of under 1.5 degrees centigrade by the year 2030. It identified progressive steps to help sustain food security through ensuring effective equitable access, building resilience across the production, processing, and distribution channels in complex food systems.

The declaration endorsed a framework for actions but acknowledged that the world food security is really under threat, especially the challenge of ensuring access to nutrition for every single person on the planet. While the global community is committed to making the right food and nutrition available to all, the declaration accepted that there are challenges and threats to the production and distribution. The question is whether there is any resilience of the system to weather the climate volatility.

It is acceptable as a fact that climate change brings not only adverse effects on food production but also possible negative impacts on human health and food security. The World Health Organization (WHO) defines such a food security matter as 'when all people at all times have access to sufficient, safe, nutritious food to maintain a healthy and active life'. WHO has recognised that climate change does play a role towards health and nutrition, and any negative repercussions will bring about nutrition insecurity and affect the livelihood of thousands.

Millions at risk

The British-based Oxfam International predicted that the number of people at risk of hunger could go up as much as 10 to 20 per cent by 2050, as the weather pattern becomes more unpredictable and one that brings with it tropical storms and floods and even droughts that would impact negatively the food production and even distribution.

The World Bank statistics are equally startling—up to 100 million people are vulnerable to extreme poverty by the year 2030. Negative impacts on health could also follow. Interestingly, the world body estimated that an increase in global temperature of 2–3°C is likely to put at risk up to 5 per cent globally, or more than 150 million people.

The World Bank report further finds the impact of extreme weather on poverty to be more devastating—702 million people are in extreme poverty due to this. According to the 2018 report on the State of Food Insecurity in the World (Sofi), 793 million people are undernourished. Climate change strikes poor and undeveloped countries even harder, compared to the rich and developed, driving the poor communities further into poverty and malnourishment. They could be living amid widespread diseases as well as shortages in food and water as climate change—droughts and change of water cycle—limits access to clean water and sanitation. Referring to the climate models, it is predicted that by 2030, the incidence of drought will increase in Central and South America, southern Europe, East and South-East Asia, and South Africa. Changing temperatures, rainfall patterns, and droughts also have devastating effects on farmers, which will lead to food insecurity.

While there is already overwhelming evidence on the effects of climate change on production, equally worrying is the adverse impacts on nutritional value. Scientists have said that rising carbon dioxide (CO_2) emissions will make the staple food crops less nutritious.

As reported in the *Guardian* newspaper, Professor Samuel Myers was quoted to have said that rising CO_2 would destroy iron and zinc, important ingredients for human health, from the tests done on wheat, rice, soybeans, and maize. Deficiencies of such minerals, according to Professor Myers, would adversely harm pregnant women and would present an enormous public health problem.

Scientist affirmation

Jessica Fanzo of Johns Hopkins University, Food and Agriculture Organization of the United Nations, in her review paper in 2018, details the effects of climate change on food system and its repercussions on nutritional values. Changes in weather patterns and intensity will affect food production and overall calorie consumption. The food supply chain across its processing, distribution, storage, and marketing will be affected, according to experts.

Changes in consumption patterns can also be due to market forces. Recent upward trend in food prices, a direct hit from changes in climate patterns, can hit the poor the hardest. Opting for the cheapest and least nutritious will be the natural reaction, and the result from this will see the poor segment of society suffer from lack of nutritional value of the food they consume—worst-case scenario is that many will suffer from obesity. In Asian countries, increase in food price will likely lead to many opting for more carbohydrate-based food, which is typically more rice, a staple diet for Asians. Studies have shown such preference run the risk of an increase in diabetes in the later part of their lives. Less-nourishing food can be especially bad for those lacking in iron and zinc; the result of this can be all sorts of illness, including weakening of immune system.

However, such a trend can also be reversed; in China, there has been an increase in meat consumption by at least sevenfold over the past four decades. Although the figures are just about a third of what US citizens consume, the trend is expected to increase. As the country's continues to enjoy higher living standards, the high-protein diet that came with it has led to increase in obesity.

The increased preference for meat consumption can itself worsen climate change conditions, where either way, increase in livestock breeding increases the energy consumption and waste discharge polluting the environment.

The answer to combat the ill effects of climate change is never an easy thing to do. Balancing between the economic and social agenda is always a tough call. But problems relating to climate change are ongoing, and many scientists will agree the biggest impacts will be those in south Sahara and parts of Asia and Africa. Rural poor will be hardest hit, and such inequity will require interventions to ensure access to food system and nutrition.

If the vision of the Rome 2014 Declaration for global action to end all forms of malnutrition is to succeed, combating climate change is obvious. But there must be a better acceptance of the linkages between climate change and nutrition among the relevant stakeholders. Despite the commitment and serious implications for food security and nutrition, various adaptation steps are necessary, and these are to be taken by each government to have a real chance to succeed.

CHAPTER 6

Sustainability and education

Felicity Healey-Benson

The Brundtland Definition (1987) of sustainability requires that humanity meet its demands today without compromising the needs of the future generation. Education for sustainable development (EfSD) is advocated as a critical means of achieving the required change to meet this challenge. Despite the recognition of the indispensability of both formal and non-formal education in changing people's attitudes, there is still much work to be done to convert policy to practice.

From core values to paradigm shift

While sustainability has gained traction as a core value in education, there is an urgent need for a more transformative approach, one that equips citizens for a VUCA (volatile, uncertain, complex and ambiguous) world, as well as averting an environmental crisis. A balance of increasing adaptive capacity to external shocks and challenges while developing the ability to assess and address sustainable development concerns.

Critique

To critique how far Education has progressed in achieving the United Nations SDGs, it is useful to assess activity through a framework lens. A means to test for authentic or deep sustainability commitment that embraces the social, the cultural, the economic, as well as the environmental is provided by leading environmental educationalists Bob Jickling and Arjen E. J. Wals.

Big Brother sustainable development

A starting block for EfSD, Big Brother sustainable development categorises a plethora of greening projects triggered by an authoritative dictate by environmental authorities or standards agencies. The role of education is to adopt and inculcate such practices. Activities range from carbon reduction, biodiversity enhancement, and buildings/campus sustainability. The Well-being of the Future Generations Act (2015) in Wales is considered a leading example, where sustainable practice is linked legislatively to the SDGs. While its intent is to revolutionise how public policy is made, fixing sustainability high on the public agenda, it's too premature to assess its impact on making any practical difference to people's lives or the planet.

Feel-good sustainable development

An uplift in focus on conforming to targets follows with improved SD literacy, and an active employ of ideas such as the triple bottom line of people-planet-profit, greening, and CSR, embedded within the curriculum and institutional management. While productive developments, critics suggest they offer educators and their learners a false sense of control over their ability to shape the future, embodying a form of greenwashing that leaves intact inherently unsustainable routines. Take the universal priority education goal for employability; links made with sustainability are predominantly incidental. Change or reform in education from early years to adult learning remains piecemeal or incremental, reductionist in orientation, and dominated by a discipline-by-discipline approach. Barriers that hinder are dispositional, situational, and institutional. Education researchers uncover lack of knowledge, lack of access to instructional materials, overcrowded curriculums, and lack of time afforded to educators, especially in systems which are heavily assessment-orientated.

Enabling thought and development beyond sustainable development

At the higher end of the spectrum, EfSD requires a focus on regenerative design and development, achieving a deeper or authentic sustainability. Bob Doppelet and William MacDonough, in their book *Leading Change toward Sustainability* (2017), claim this can only be achieved through transformative learning supported by transformative pedagogy. To operationalise, teaching approaches must focus on elements relating to the processes of learning and on the development of capabilities to improvise, adapt, innovate, and create. Fourth Industrial Revolution skills such as interdisciplinary thinking, problem solving, team-working, and critical and holistic thinking are key. Educational institutions should be more focused on supporting people to reflect critically or endeavour creatively to redress what is happening to the planet, to dedicate the space for alternative mechanisms from those that have fed the economic forces of consumerism. This inevitability calls for a much higher level of investment of time, attention, resources, and thought.

Interdependent and interconnected

For UNESCO, a key approach to EfSD is intercultural education, '*nurturing respect for, and appreciation of diversity cannot be realized without adhering to democratic values and practices*', a requisite for a just society where everyone's participation in social, cultural, economic, and political life is valued and counted. When students engage internationally with other students, they gradually learn to develop intercultural competencies. This requires a far more ambitious cross-educational strategy than experienced to date, that develops learners who are willing and capable of considering global problems and other people's perspectives and behaviours from multiple viewpoints. The adoption of the new global competence assessment developed by OECD through its Programme for International Student Assessment (PISA) is hoped to drive the requisite future behaviours in education.

Innovation, creativity, and interdisciplinarity

Over twenty years ago, Sir Ken Robinson argued that education at all levels squanders creativity and innovation. In 2019, despite a consensus of the importance of creativity and innovation in our educational institutions around the world, internal cultures remain quite resistant to change and innovation, heavily focused on assessment. The mindsets of the educators and the autonomy they are given to adapt are also crucial. Last year, delegates drawn from more than 100 countries visited Qatar for the global World Innovation Summit for Education (WISE) and identified the initiatives they believe will drive innovation and creativity forward. They included artificial intelligence, leveraging social entrepreneurship for innovation, reimagining higher education in the connected world, and connecting private and public actors to build future knowledge societies. Worldwide research also provides the evidence that when students are taught to conduct rigorous research, they learn to become increasingly comfortable when dealing with unstructured and ill-defined problems. When educators can develop multidisciplinary perspectives or adopt an interdisciplinary approach to their programmes, they are unleashing the innovative and creative potential to challenge engrained economic models. Yet all these are intentional strategies and processes; they will not be achieved through osmosis. True sustainability built on creativity, innovation, and interdisciplinarity demands time, sponsorship, and investment.

Early start

While a lot of attention is placed on graduates with the right skills and mindsets, sustainability must be embedded from early years' education, the stage when children develop their basic values, attitudes, skills, behaviours, and habits, which may be long lasting. This must be beyond the rediscovery of the outdoors, promoting the wonder and respect of nature, but support engagement in intellectual dialogue and concrete actions in favour of the environment. As highlighted by UNESCO, even the very young can be encouraged to question overconsumption through discussions about familiar food products, clothes, toys, and advertisements: *'Such discussions could be expanded to incorporate considerations about their counterparts in less materially rich circumstances and stimulate conversations about solidarity and co-operation.'*

Key challenges

While there is much to celebrate and praise in the achievements made with SDGs across the world within education, the cold fact is that more needs to be done. Two key challenges disrupt the pace and depth of change.

Challenge #1: Prevailing individualist capitalist system

Despite the growing numbers of educational pioneers, innovators, social pirates, and activists rallying together to lead the way in authentic sustainability activity, many are dangerously enslaved by the capitalist system of education itself. Fundamentally, education is designed not so much as collective social good but traded as an individual good and a commodity on the global education market. The battle for educational prestige by institutes themselves has driven also driven up the cost of education. Furthermore, linear thinking patterns, silo-working, and hierarchies indicative of the traditional education institutions are increasingly ill-suited to address the exponentially increasing complexity of the modern world.

Collaborative and creative working methods, networks, and systemic approaches are urgently needed to encourage the holistic thinking required. Peter Senge, a major proponent of systemic change in education, argues this would help all stakeholders appreciate that individual actions impact and contribute to an interconnected system that determines both the well-being of humans and the planet.

Biomimicry, coined as 'innovation inspired by nature' by Janine Benyus, is also a key model for adoption. Perfectly aligned to transdisciplinarity, biomimicry can respond to the increasing demand for relevance and applicability of all types of research to societal challenges. As one example, lecturers (Dr Sandra Dettmer, Shellie Holden, and Katherine Clewett) from the departments of Art and Business at the Swansea Business School (UWTSD) created a multidisciplinary Creative Test Space for their Art and Business students. This enables their students to work collaboratively to adopt and embed the element of circularity into product or service design processes and business models. Consequently, students have been able to extend products and materials value for longer, with waste and resource use minimised.

The challenge to the system was even more pronounced when a group of schoolchildren in the city of Kuala Lumpur were caught at the centre of controversy over a play depicting the scenario of disappearing orangutan, from deforestation. According to the *Star* news report on 2 July 2019, these students were attempting to demonstrate the orangutan would disappear from forests if palm oil is not sustainably grown and cultivated. The young students in environmentally themed costumes were told it would be a disservice to the nation's palm oil industry.

Sustainability has also appeared in mainstream education or as a core elective in most leading business schools. While more students may be now more aware of the importance of ecological and social responsibilities, integrating these into profit-centred industries is more challenging. To begin with, there are not many 'chief sustainability officer' posts to go around. Business continues to use sustainability as one of their main drivers, but main elements of sustainable development remains, at best, nice to have. More needs to be done to facilitate a deeper integration and application of sustainable development principles into core business, across end-to-end processes, from design and production to delivery.

The concept and application of the circular economy must replace the dominating linear approach, where waste is given least attention, and material used for production is based on the lowest cost. If education is to have a more meaningful impact, especially at tertiary level, the whole concept of the business model must change.

Challenge #2: Resourcing crisis

One would be challenged to disprove that there are increasing funding pressures within education. Learning crises are not just reported in countries such as the UK and the USA. The UNESCO Institute for Statistics (UIS) reports on 617 million children and adolescents globally as not proficient in reading, writing, or doing mathematics. Cuts to education budgets have resulted in a higher ratio of teachers to learners than ever experienced, detrimental cuts to curriculum provision, including loss of music, arts, and sports, teachers self-financing key resources and materials, and technology, text, and material shortfalls—all with harmful impacts on content access, staff and learner well-being, and support needed for learners to succeed.

Children with wealthy parents or access to heavily resourced schools, however benevolent the benefactors are, are the ones most likely to succeed in the system. The education system in many countries, more so in emerging countries, remains inadequately funded, inequitably distributed. These issues fundamentally undermine the SDGs.

SDGs are unlikely to be achieved if most of the signatories from the developing countries do not start from ground up. It must be remembered that the impact of climate change, including nutrition, food security, and even unpredictable weathers will hit the poor the most. But governments in these markets are ill prepared, and they have an obligation to build capacity and educating schools to embrace the concept and goals of sustainable development.

A key to successful innovation and less duplication of limited resources is partnership and alliances through increased use of global networks for the educators, the learners, the leadership, and all key stakeholders. This should also extend to business and industrial partnerships so that there is a true collaborate to co-create solutions for more dynamic sustainability challenges and opportunities. Networks of peers can feed the creative co-production of new knowledge more productively. Better educational professional practice being key to the transformation of the teaching profession will facilitate the achievement of the SDGs. Global sponsors must also be well resourced and governed to ensure resources are kept distributed to stay focused, and outcomes are well aligned.

On being radical or naive, if it quickens the pace for societal transformation

Greta Thunberg, the Swedish teenage environmentalist, has been criticised as being naive in her endeavours to call out the lack of real action towards addressing climate change. Interestingly, she represents a growing zeitgeist of empowerment movements that reach far beyond the address of accelerating environmental degradation, which bites at the heels of traditional power systems. She produced a sixty-page book questioning why societies and governments are ignoring global warming warnings from majority of scientists. She only focused on one single issue—climate warming. She was right to point out it would be her responsibility in expressing concern over her future. But educating sustainability will require more than what the young Greta has expressed.

Politics aside, the indigestible fact of the matter is that just under half the world's wealth is in the hands of just 1 per cent of the population (Credit Suisse, 2018). Free and fresh thinking is paramount to motivate and harness the power of individuals, groups, and institutions to redress several imbalances across the world which are contributing *to* unsustainable development practices and future emerging risks. In the words of Professor Lummina Horlings, 'transformation to sustainability is not only driven by practices and political structures, but also by beliefs, values, worldviews and paradigms that influence attitudes and actions.'

Indeed, such views in changing lifestyle ought to be embraced, from being a champion in words and actions through to changes in production and consumption behaviours. This demands some sacrifices of lifestyle that would include, for example, reduction of meat and holidays abroad, and adoption of reduction and reuse behaviours.

Foe and/or friend

Education is the foe and the friend of sustainability. Education as a key function of stability or pattern maintenance in society is now incongruent with its responsibility to be a key driver of global change. Holistic thinking, collaborative learning, a praxis and problematic-solving orientation, and a networked stakeholder base will be integral to EfSD delivering an ecosystem-orientated pedagogy aimed at authentic sustainability.

UNESCO is right to push for an education agenda that integrates key sustainable development issues into education and learning. Across the wide and often complex issues of climate change, food security, nutrition, poverty elimination, gender, etc., the execution of such agenda matters. Raising awareness is one thing, but embracing a change in culture, values, habits, and behaviours requires collaboration and recognition. No one wants to sacrifice if others won't. A concerted global effort requires leadership and commitment. In doing so, the design of the education system must be one that is genuinely transformative if it is to succeed in developing the sustainable mindsets that will co-create or co-resolve global wicked problems for conjoined human and environmental benefit for generations to come.

CHAPTER 7

Gender inequality and sustainability

Published statistics available on gender inequality in political, economic, and social participation are startling.

- A World Bank report states that there is easily a total of 150 countries in the world today that do not give equal rights to women.
- From the same World Bank report, there are no laws against domestic violence.
- According to Inter Parliamentary Union, women are under-represented in national parliaments in most countries.
- The WEF reports that globally twelve million girls get married before the age of 18, in other words, thirty-three thousand daily or one every two seconds.
- Only 52 per cent of women married or in a union freely make their own decisions about sexual relations, contraceptive use, and health care.

- In the rural parts of Africa, women spend forty billion hours annually just to collect water.
- In eighteen countries, husbands can legally prevent their wives from working; in thirty-nine countries, daughters and sons do not have equal inheritance right.

Issues

The annual World Economic Forum (WEF) that brings together hundreds of global leaders has said it would take 108 years to close the gender gap. In its Global Gender Gap Report first published in 2006, it produces the Global Gender Gap Index covering 144 major and emerging economies. The highest possible score is a one, meaning equality or better for women. No countries had such a score even in the advanced nations where the gap is closer.

WEF takes a strong stand on its commitment to raise awareness on gender issues but also to influence world leaders to reverse the trend or at least to close the gaps in both economic and social standing of women. In its 2018 research on gender inequality, WEF has highlighted issues on child marriages—globally, the survey shows twelve million girls get married before they turn 18, legal status where only a handful of countries (six) actually recognise women's legal rights as equal to their men counterparts', and even in the field of science and technology, WEF found that only 22 per cent of the world's artificial-intelligence professionals are women. Importantly, WEF's survey showed improvement in women having more access to education and job opportunities.

McKinsey Global Institute Research produced a similar study on gender inequality in 2015, revealing that the world had 655 million fewer women in the labour force than men, but they spent three times the amount of time on unpaid domestic work at home. Even more worrying is that there are 195 million women less literate than men, and a similar number do not have a bank account. In one of their conclusions in the study, McKinsey found that women could potentially add as much as USD28 trillion to world's output if they were given the opportunities in both education and employment.

Gender inequality is obvious across workplace, home, and community, but there are differences. Such concern is not only historical, but women make up half the world's population. Studies continue to show majority of women are in lower-paying jobs, or they are paid less even if they are in the same job requiring the same level of expertise and contributions. In many markets, they do not have equal access to employment opportunities. While steps have been taken to close the gaps, with much success in developed markets, gender inequality in economic and social developments persist in majority of the emerging countries.

SD goals

Gender equality is one of seventeen UN Sustainable Development Goals (SDGs). The UN SDGs were established to uphold the fairness, justice, and human rights aim through fairer access for women to opportunities. One of the seventeen UN Sustainable Development Goals, gender equality (number 5) is devoted to removing gender inequality through empowering of women and girls across all its economic and social programmes and activities. The mission on gender equality has a goal to achieve by 2030; it is committed to assist so that in all parts of the world, where progress is concerned, no women should be left behind.

Studies undertaken by international agencies have consistently showed that giving women and ensuring gender equality is necessary to support sustainable development. It is also morally the right thing to do, as ending all forms of discrimination against women and gender is also a plus point and multiplier effect on both the economies as well as the social developments.

UNDP

There are already a number of programme initiatives undertaken by international agencies, especially those from the United Nations. These are not easy to overcome as the United Nations recognises the problems of women and girls being subject to widespread discrimination and violence, especially in cultures where women are treated differently. In many cases, United Nations agencies have a challenge of reversing centuries-old, deep-rooted culture of gender bias and openly making gender equality a fundamental human right, a necessary foundation for a peaceful, prosperous, and sustainable world.

The chances of such goal being achieved are challenging, given that the UN statistics show that one in five women and girls between the ages of 15 and 49 have reported experiencing physical or sexual violence by an intimate partner within a twelve-month period, and forty-nine countries currently have no laws protecting women from domestic violence. The international community, however, has raised better awareness on traditional practices such as child marriage; there is still a long way before such practices can become a thing of the past.

To an extent, there has been considerable success in these projects; for example, the United Nations Development

Programme in emerging countries reported considerable success in increasing the number of girls attending schools, and gender employment across many economic sectors. Ensuring equal access will not happen overnight. In many places, women continue to be exploited in both opportunities and pay. Reports of sexual violence and child marriage across South Asia and the Middle East, however, are worrying.

But UNDP has rolled out a project with private-sector Gender Equality Seal Certification partnering some 400 companies in Latin America that has helped to eliminate gender pay gaps, guided many to increase women's roles in decision-making and communication, and raised awareness and capacity in fighting sexual harassment at work.

UNICEF

The United Nations International Children's Emergency Fund (UNICEF), for example, recognises the challenge of addressing gender inequality. From community perceptions to institutions, one of these includes stereotyping of women's roles in societies. UNICEF knows that to overcome these challenges means removing generational changes and giving girls higher ambitions and challenges.

UNICEF invests in technology to (1) build capacity among the local communities to empower women and (2) help youths to shape their confidence through skills development, education, and training. By focusing on low-income economies in the Middle East, South Asia, and poorer nations in Latin America, UNICEF aims to help local partners to invest in girls' skills for employability, especially vocational and technical.

Providing women and girls with equal access to education, health care, decent work, and representation in political and economic decision-making processes will fuel sustainable economies and benefit societies and humanity at large. Implementing new legal frameworks regarding female equality in the workplace and the eradication of harmful practices targeted at women is crucial to ending the gender-based discrimination prevalent in many countries around the world.

Change

Statistics show in many economies, women have achieved considerable success across many fields, including both political and corporate leadership. But across all societies, progress towards gender equality is slow and inconsistent. There may be women CEOs in many global corporations and international agencies, but overall, statistics show women continue to be under-represented and gender pay gap is still considerable. Women also tend to have shorter careers, as many opt to go part-time to devote time for raising children.

Sociologists regard gender inequality as a consequence of very deeply rooted societal bias associated with both sexes, with females being weaker, passive, and confined to homemaking and child rearing. Both boys and girls are brought up socially differently; even their roles in society are stereotypes and confined to domestic homes. During the industrial age, such perceptions remain deeply rooted that women's roles are restricted to those jobs that are typically paid lower. This continues even when women have moved up to be as capable, and despite performing the same, majority are seemingly paid less.

An OECD report showed that despite efforts by governments to address gender inequality, progress has been slow and uneven. One reason is the entrenched social and cultural norms that continue to maintain the bias and, hence, discrimination. The OECD report also points out that in advanced nations, such gender stereotypes are hindering progress in enforcement of policies, leading to limited access for women to leadership positions. Improvements to gaps in income areas have been slow.

Even in places (for example, the European Union) where legislations on gender equality have been far more advanced than elsewhere, statistics on gender inequality are still very glaring. Despite the business case of addressing gender inequality, McKinsey in their studies showed efforts to close the gap will take years, but adoption of the sustainable development goals remains the right thing to do. This will require, however, significant investment and concerted efforts to ensure the other half are not left behind.

CHAPTER 8

Water challenges

It is a scary thought to even suggest that the biggest challenge facing humanity is not political differences but water scarcity. There is empirical evidence of such concern that the United Nations has recognised access to clean water as a human right. Access to water is a sustainability concern to all stakeholders, including communities, businesses, and governments.

There is already competition for such water access that will pit businesses head-on against the growing populations for such diminishing resources. It is only a matter of time that nations will eventually go into conflict for such precious resources, noticeably where nations share the same source of water supplies. The examples of such countries are those in the Middle East, Pakistan-India, and China-Vietnam.

Indeed, there are already external factors beyond government control, so multilateral agencies put this as a high alert. Water is at the heart of sustainable development; it is one of the major contributors towards health, development, and humanity. Availability of clean water has contributed to a broad range of socioeconomic developments, often under-recognised; it is unthinkable to imagine the world without water.

No one disagrees that water is a finite and irreplaceable resource. Water can be recycled, but it is very costly. Yet many take it for granted. Many nations are blessed with such resources; their people probably don't even realise how lucky they are to have piped water available to them 24/7. Those who live in high rainfall regions may not even know that more than a billion people on earth do not have such access. Today there are almost two billion people living in places where depletion of water has reached a level where they no longer can be assured of daily access to water. Water is therefore part of sustainable development, and it must be managed efficiently and responsibly to help balance the adverse effects on the fragile ecosystem.

The importance of water in sustainable development is also an essential part of public health, failing which the risk of many, including children, falling ill or even dying from diseases associated with inadequate water supply and hygiene.

Reports of water scarcity and inadequate sanitation have negatively impacted food security and threaten the fragile societies where the poor lack access. There are now at least more than a billion people who are vulnerable to diseases due to water scarcity. There are also recorded cases of prolonged droughts which have brought about hunger and malnutrition.

Much investment has been made to better manage water resources and sanitation systems.

To improve sanitation and access to drinking water, there needs to be increased investment in management of freshwater ecosystems and sanitation facilities on a local level in several developing countries within sub-Saharan Africa, Central Asia, South Asia, East Asia, and South-East Asia.

Shortages

The United Nations Food and Agriculture Organization (FAO), in one of its reports, said forty-five countries were experiencing water shortages, defined as less than a thousand cubic metres (one million litres) per person a year. These countries include South Africa, Cyprus, and Morocco. A few others, especially Middle East countries with surging population growth, including Algeria, Israel, and Qatar, are already in a dangerous zone with looming extreme shortage with less than 500 m^3 per person a year.

Vietnam will face water shortage in a report made at a 2019 forum on water resource management. The country, with a population of 90 million, has an average surface volume of about 830 billion, but two thirds come from neighbouring countries, according to a report by Asia News Network. The country faces water shortage because of pollution in the rivers and groundwater. Just as in elsewhere, Vietnam's reliance on groundwater faces risk of overuse and mismanagement.

In response to the diminishing water from traditional sources, more than a third of world's population depends on groundwater and the UN has warned of the danger of overusing these reserves. In some parts of Asia, including India, groundwater reserves have come to the rescue to many communities, as well as those in Italy, Greece, and Spain.

Drying cities

Cape Town became the first city that has gone completely dry after years of drought. It is not the first to experience this; in 2014, Sao Paulo in Brazil recorded the worst drought in history. The overcrowded city of twenty million often experiences extreme water shortages due to little rainfall and deforestation of the Amazon.

But Cape Town in South Africa ran out of fresh water for its four million citizens on 15 July 2018. The tragedy is that with proper planning and effective early interventions, this crisis could have been averted. Many experts believe that warning bells were heard as early as 1990, but now Cape Town may have the dubious distinction of being the first major developed city calling in the military to keep the peace over water scarcity.

The global use of fresh water doubled between 1964 and 2014 because of population growth, urbanisation, industrialisation, and increased production and consumption, the UN says. The demand for water in cities is expected to grow by 50 per cent by 2030. 'Water scarcity, exacerbated by climate change, could cost some regions up to 6 per cent of their GDP, spur migration, and spark conflict,' the World Bank said in 2016.

Troubled farming

Farming is the single biggest consumer of water globally (70 per cent), most of it for irrigation. Industry uses 19 per cent and households 11 per cent, according to the FAO (FAO).

But there are wide disparities at the regional level. In South Asia, agriculture accounts for 91 per cent of water use, against only 7 per cent in homes and 2 per cent in industry.

In the European Union and North America, however, industry consumes more than half of freshwater supply, ahead of agriculture (under 34 per cent) and domestic use (under 18 per cent).

Global warming

The UN's climate science panel, the Intergovernmental Panel on Climate Change (IPCC), said in a 2014 report that for every degree Celsius of global warming, about 7 per cent of the world's population will see a drop of at least 20 per cent in renewable water resources.

The IPCC projects more frequent and severe droughts in already dry regions, reducing surface water and groundwater stocks. The impact will depend on the level of warming, according to a 2016 American Geophysical Union (AGU) conference with UN FAO, IPCC, UN-Water, and the World Bank. The conference reiterated the message that the world has abundant fresh water, but it is unevenly distributed and under increasing pressure. One example is the severe shortages in Cape Town.

Water reserves

More than 97 per cent of the planet's water is salty, most of it in the oceans and seas, but there is also a good supply of fresh water.

Every year, an estimated 42.8 trillion cubic metres of renewable fresh water circulates as rain, surface water, or groundwater, according to the UN's FAO. This equals 16,216 litres per person per day—four times the amount required in the United States, for example, for personal and domestic consumption, industry, and agriculture. Depending on diet and lifestyle, a person needs between 2,000 and 5,000 litres of water a day to produce their food and meet their drinking and sanitation requirements, the FAO says.

About 60 per cent of the planet's freshwater reserves is locked in the Antarctic. Of the rest, more than a quarter is in Central and Latin America, which is sixty times more than that available in the Middle East and North Africa.

'The fact is there is enough water to meet the world's growing needs, but not without dramatically changing the way water is used, managed and shared. The global water crisis is one of governance,' the United Nations said in 2015.

Water pollution is one of the reasons behind water shortage. Large-scale farming with the use of pesticides and fertilisers that are washed into the rivers plus human waste or industrial waste has made the problem of river pollution much worse. Much of the rivers which traditionally supply fresh water became contaminated, and clean-up of such environmental hazards will take years.

Agricultural activities, while posing a threat to the environment, use easily more than 50 per cent of the world's water resources. The large irrigation systems used for cultivation of crops have often been blamed for excessive use and water wastage. Rising populations have also added stress on the system, resulting in use of water drying out rivers, lakes, and underground aquifers. There are countries which have devoted much of their resources to agricultural activities. Examples like India, China, Australia, or the United States are already stretching their limits on water consumption.

Population pressure

Population growth is another challenge. The rise in population, often at places where access to resources is scarce, has worsened the conditions. One of these is water scarcity, which can lead to additional negative impacts on the local public health, the number of people suffering hunger, and the development of the population.

Developments on diminishing resources add pressure on ecosystems, one of which is the fast disappearance of wetlands that are essential for animals and plants, including the agriculture. Despite these impacts, ecosystems will be in danger because natural landscapes can dry out, change, or be polluted.

Additionally, economies can decline without enough water. To sum up, the natural resource water, especially fresh water, is already scarce because of water pollution, agriculture, and population growth. Even though some countries are not affected yet, everyone should be alarmed and be thoughtful when using any kind of water. Urgent action is needed if we are to avoid a global water crisis.

But this issue of water scarcity and preparedness isn't just limited to Cape Town. It could happen to any of the crowded cities. No one likes inconveniences of having a day without access to clean water, whether by drinking, washing, or eating food, all of which depend on water. There is an urgent need for better water conservation; message and meaning should be better understood, because water scarcity can and will affect larger populations nearly anywhere on the planet. In any given year, at least 3.4 billion people globally are susceptible to freshwater scarcity. That's scary.

CHAPTER 9

Ethical dimension of business

Globalisation of businesses has led to convergence of rules and governance, standards and practice. Businesses that have grown and expanded in global markets are constantly in search of cost efficiency. This means more outsourcing opportunities of their non-core activities to local suppliers, often across global markets.

The past decades witnessed a relocation trend of foreign production closer to the source of raw materials. This trend comes with the need to manage different stakeholders with different cultures and habits. It also means a greater challenge to ensure compliance with local regulation and respect for local customs and practices.

Although no one wants to be reminded of the infamous cases of Nike in Indonesia or Shell in Nigeria, cases of unethical practices involving multinational companies (MNCs) are not uncommon. It is even a bigger challenge when it comes to making sure the outsourcing service providers that are comprised of largely small- to medium-sized enterprises (SME) adopt good corporate responsibility practices. Many

MNCs are aware that their reputation can be on the line if one of their SME suppliers breaks the rules. For example, Mattel learned expensive lessons when their products made by their suppliers were found to have failed the minimum health and safety tests in US markets.

To overcome such challenges, it is not uncommon to find big companies issuing guidelines to monitor the behaviours of their SME suppliers. It is therefore not uncommon for multinationals to review regularly the practices of their SME partners across global operations, as such preliminary risk assessments can help to identify issues and potential problems, be they environmentally or socially irresponsible practices.

Environment

Environmental-based issues are now integral parts of the larger companies. This explains why larger global firms are now insisting that the wider sustainability agenda be understood and embraced by the smaller suppliers in order to protect their brand image from adverse pressure groups or media.

For example, Toyota and General Motors in the auto industry do demand that their suppliers have an environmental management system or at least provide minimum level of environment quality standard. In Britain, large supermarket chain stores Marks & Spencer and Sainsbury's go a step further to insist that their suppliers embrace ethical and social issues such as wage levels, working hours, and health and safety, and now it is common for them to demand fair-trade label as part of their sustainable development practices.

Many multinationals do get their risk managers to ensure their suppliers comply to self-assessment questionnaires, and such ticking the boxes will then be followed up with on-site audits. It is a common practice to find the large companies managing such an improvement process through regular dialogues and reviews with their suppliers. In some cases, large companies do insist that their suppliers use environmentally friendly products in their production and packaging. It is also common now for suppliers to accept a code of conduct that requires adoption of good business practices. Best practices in vendor management now include allocation of management time to educate and train vendors on work ethics, energy savings, recycling, and environment care across work performed by the suppliers. The larger suppliers are now required to acquire international standards, from environment to employment practices. Even customer education on environment awareness, including proper labelling, has become a trend.

The supplier relationship does not guarantee SME suppliers will be free from any unethical practices, and it is impossible for the larger companies to monitor all social and environmental issues because of the complexity of the supply chain management, especially in cases where the suppliers themselves could also outsource their production or procurement to third parties. There is also the issue of cost competitiveness, and many of these suppliers must rely on their second- or third-tier suppliers to retain their cost competitiveness.

This is where the challenge is. A higher number of human resource issues, environmental pollution, and health and safety violations tend to be found in smaller companies, especially further down the supply chain. Many SME suppliers are family owned. Many of these owners have found that starting up a business can be a daunting process. Indeed, many will treat spending money on safety gear, pollution controls, and corporate governance as the last things on their to-do list. Indeed, there may even be some SME owners who would rather pay fines than invest in environmental and social capital!

Their management systems can often be inadequate; although having an ISO-certified management system is not difficult to achieve, it is no guarantee that actual management control and performance can be noticeably better. Occupational health and safety and product governance are often key areas where weakness can be discovered.

Smaller enterprises

Recent studies show that many small to medium enterprises demonstrated a reactive approach to CSR, with management systems only implemented at the request of large customers. As in most cases, legislative requirements were the principal driver, unlike their multinational partners whose big brands have helped to put corporate responsibility at the forefront of their business agenda. But it is the small to medium business sector that is still lagging, and it is this sector that can make a big difference.

SMEs worldwide account for more than 85 per cent of businesses and 60–70 per cent of employment in OECD economies. They could account for more than 30 per cent of the country's gross domestic product. SMEs also account for more than half the country's working population. They also influence local communities, provide jobs and business entrepreneurship for the less well-off, and make up a key part of community life.

Compliance trends

Although studies on the attitudes of SMEs towards concept and application of its corporate social responsibility

(CSR) are country based, it is widely believed that majority of these SME owners will overwhelmingly see such responsibility practice as an additional effort but so long as these will bring about improved efficiency, they will welcome the idea that good corporate responsibility behaviour is good for SME business. A number of their leaders do support and advocate responsible entrepreneurship, clean-and-green initiatives, and employee health and safety. Majority will agree as a necessary compliance rather than view it from an ethical perspective.

It is, however, an acceptable point that having a strong ethical dimension can help SME entrepreneurs to differentiate their products or services from competitors. Indeed, this is one of the fundamental principles of running a successful business, i.e. a competitive advantage. Eco-friendly products can help in product differentiation, and energy efficiency helps drive cost down. With increasing cost of energy and waste management, it does make business sense to go green.

Many changes will be expected as SMEs will start putting in place codes of conduct, policy documents, or even employee engagement programmes. SMEs may not see these as CSR activities but more as their business efficiency or a need to go with the regulators' demands. The ethical demands may not be seen in the same light as the larger MNCs'.

Globalisation can be a boon to sustainability—good ethical practices can help fuel and influence local SME suppliers. To make this work, the ethical dimension must be aligned to the business practices and be a contributor to profitability of their business. Driving such performance requires positive engagement that includes a good business case and practical tools and support to help in the process. In the final analysis, this could be the missing jigsaw piece to complete supply chain best practice.

CHAPTER 10

Sustainability in the fashion business

When a documentary video made by the People for the Ethical Treatment of Animals (PETA) was uploaded in 2015, many viewers were appalled and caught unaware of the cruel process being deployed. Today the Birkin bags are a luxury; each of them would require skins from three crocodiles, retailing at no less than US$30,000 and all the way up to a quarter of a million US dollars.

Cruelty for vanity

It is equally horrifying to know that animals confined in cramped cages are being cruelly killed for their fur. China today is the world's largest producer of fur for the high-end clothing industry. Each year, more than 100 million animals— some are bred for their fur, while others captured in the wild are often skinned for their fur. Up to thirty-five foxes die just to make a fur coat. Beavers, muskrats, and even bears are trapped in the wild, suffering in huge pain before they die.

Even in developed markets such as Canada, United Kingdom, and United States, it is not uncommon to find sheep in the farm shorn cruelly for their wool and seals in the wild being clubbed to death for their fur. Many of these fur workers resort to using the cheapest method, often the most painful, to carry out their daily acts.

Whether the finished goods are a fur coat or a handbag, the removal of natural skin or fur caused tremendous suffering; it is one of those sustainability issues where both retailers and consumers are being challenged on their ethical values, and beliefs.

The fashion business is huge. The annual turnover is worth easily more than one trillion US dollars. The industry employs hundreds of millions of jobs across its supply chain around the world. In textiles alone, China along with Bangladesh, Vietnam, and India are the biggest clothes makers in the world. China alone produces one fifth of the world's garment output for some of the top brands that include Nike, H & M, Zara, Adidas, Uniqlo.

The industry enjoys a phenomenal growth fuelled by world demand. Boston Consulting Group is predicting the growth to be as high as 63 per cent in overall fashion consumption from the period 2017 to 2030.

According to the McKinsey Global Fashion Index, the industry has grown 5.5 per cent annually. In the US alone, a total of US250 billion is spent annually on fashion alone. Rising consumerism has meant more and more people cannot resist buying more clothes or fashion accessories than they need. Rising fashion consciousness coupled with growing affluence across both developed and emerging markets partly explains the growth.

This success has not only come with a huge ethical issue on cruelty to animals but equally important, the environmental cost.

Sales pressure

To begin with, fashion today is on a fast track; shorter shelf life has meant that turnover of retail sales must be high to sustain profitability. The increase in sales volumes that demand higher production means a growing carbon footprint, mainly increased use of toxic chemicals and waste from textile production. For example, environmentalists are already complaining of rapid rise in ecological harmful plastic microfibres from polyester fabrics being part of the wastes making their way into the fragile ecosystem of the oceans.

Today, polyester has become a favourite fabric used for all occasions, but when these garments are put to wash, they produce microfibres that will end up as waste, which eventually will find its way to the ocean, posing a threat to aquatic ecosystems. Additionally, rise in demand for fast clothing also entails a higher demand for natural fabrics, for example, cotton. The growing of cotton requires much water, and unfortunately, it means a bigger water footprint putting greater stress on the cotton-producing countries of India and Egypt.

Environmental impacts

The production and distribution of the crops and synthetic fibres used for garments of all categories are net contributors to pollution in not only water, but also air and soil. It was reported in the CBS news.com on 30 November 2017 that the industry generates 1.26 billion tons of greenhouse emissions annually, even more than that of both shipping and international flights combined. Even worse is the industry only recycles 1 per cent of its material, and half a million tons of plastic microfibres end up in the ocean.

Over the years, the fashion and apparel industry has slowly accepted that sustainability is good for its business. The industry is very aware of its significant impact due to the size of its business. It employs more than sixty million people across its global value chain.

The push towards a greener environment is also consumer driven. In a recent interview, Lou Stoppard, a fashion journalist, highlighted a survey that shows nearly half of consumers prefer to purchase their clothing from companies that care about the environment. This comes mostly from the younger generations, who are passionate over environmental concerns, as well as their acceptance of recycling and reused apparel. In the US, the market is expected to reach USD64 billion by the year 2028.

Changes

Acceptance of a more sustainable business has not come without much effort from non-governmental organisations such as PETA, which has successfully run protest using famous names or even controversial slogans to bring attention of consumers. Focusing on four key areas that targeted factory farms, clothing and apparel, the entertainment industry, and animal research labs, PETA spent much time talking to and persuading leading industry players. Getting the fashion retailers has taken much longer time than expected; PETA innovated, often targeting owners.

In 2005, they successfully persuaded Inditex Group, owner of Zara, to ban the sale of fur-related products in all their 100-plus outlets. Many retail distributors such as Forever

21, JC Penney, Timberland, and many American brands have given their pledge. Using scare tactics helps to some extent, but the challenge is now extended to emerging counties with growing affluent populations in Asia, the Middle East, and Eastern Europe.

Despite rising consumer awareness across the globe, made much easier through social media and YouTube, many complaints on the fashion industry persist. Still, from the sustainability perspective, they need to start from the supply chain. The complexity of outsourcing activities it is often a lengthy process to get down to the source where it all began. Specific targets on reducing the impacts include policies on cruelty to animals, and standards as well as alternative sources should be clear. There is also a need to change work culture and consumer attitudes and behaviours. This sounds good, but it is often notoriously difficult to get consumer attention on sustainability issues.

Fashion companies have responded well to alternative materials to combat environmental issues as well as, to some extent, use less animal fur or hides. They will also find such potential across the value chain. An example is C & A, a Dutch-based retailer which introduced a 'cradle-to-cradle certified' T-shirt at mass-market price, with the use of sustainable polyester. The concept is based on incorporating the sustainability concept into their end-to-end value chain and product lifestyle. H & H, another global retailer, has adopted a longer shelf life concept in its design and quality. A similar concept being promoted carries the message to consumers 'buy less, choose well, make it last'. Accordingly, making the shelf life of clothes three months longer could help with 3 per cent of water, waste, and carbon impacts in the supply chain.

While technical and process innovations have made incremental differences, the concept of recycling of fibres has been stepped up. For example, the Ellen MacArthur Foundation introduced the Circular Fibres Initiative, which brought together the relevant industry stakeholders closer to the circular economy for textiles. The foundation considers the adoption of circular economy could help save more than 160 billion euros by 2030. To some extent, Marks & Spencer believe they could increase recycling activities by allowing customers to drop their used clothes at their retail stores. The trend of using the retail outlets as collection points for recycling purposes has also captured the interest of Zara in their stores in China. H & M has gone one step further to introduce a renewal of used clothes through their Newcell and Eileen Fisher's Renew programmes.

A significant impact is the availability of mass-production technologies which have made fibre recycling become more cost-effective. This helps to recycle the waste fabrics into useful materials. These developments are very much in response to help meet the challenge of a shopaholic society that takes fast fashion for granted and uses cheap clothes as part of its throwaway attitude. A large percentage of the apparel ends up in landfills; even worse still, according to the United Nations Economic Commission for Europe, 40 per cent of these are never worn.

Another player in the sustainability movement is the Danish Fashion Institute (DFI), which has an agenda on awareness on sustainability in the fashion industry. DFI collaborates with global brands to drive sustainability agenda. This includes H & M, Target, Li & Fung, and the Sustainable Apparel Coalition among a few to connect with suppliers with sustainability prescriptions. The agenda originated in the feedback from their diverse stakeholders on pains and the ugly side of their fashion business. The movement has produced a to-do list in their sustainability agenda; among these are to improve transparency of supply chain activities, especially on the source of materials, including raw materials and geographies. Priorities were also focused on efficiency towards use of water and energy, but more importantly the use of chemicals. While these may not eliminate completely the level of pollution and carbon emission, data and intelligence would help its collaborators with the chance to reduce and recycle. There are also priorities in the list of improvements that include innovation in material used, where organic cotton and newer sustainable materials are being introduced.

The Fast Retailing Company, the world's third largest apparel manufacturer and retailer, has started its campaign to switch from plastic bags to eco-friendly paper bags as part of its priorities for sustainability. The group, which carries fast-growing brands such as Uniqlo, publicly announced its new labour and environmental standards. By adopting new innovations in the production, the company wants to cut down water usage and waste by 90 per cent. The company has made it clear that sustainability is fully integrated into their business model in both production and retail.

G-Star Raw, the Dutch designer clothing company based in Amsterdam, in its 2019 sustainability report, is fully committed to its sustainability strategy, an outcome from its extensive consultation with its stakeholders, including employees, suppliers, and customers. The company has defined its sustainability initiatives that range from embracing the Global Fashion Agenda to Zero Discharge of Hazardous Chemicals Initiatives and the Sustainable Apparel Coalition. This requires the company to be committed to embrace circular processes, ensure transparency, and help innovate sustainable development in its people and business.

The wide sustainability agenda further gives attention to improvement in work conditions of outsourcing companies. But more important is the opportunity to introduce and share new technologies which do not only help improve work conditions but also reduce energy consumption, hence the carbon footprint of older technologies.

Recent developments have not only raised awareness but also improved the environmental and social performance of the fashion industry. While it is recognised that much needs to be done, there is an agreement that the industry has a responsibility to lead and raise awareness on issues that range from cruelty to animals to environmental matters.

Environmental and social stress from the fashion industry nonetheless will not disappear overnight. Consumer behaviours will need to change if the industry needs to adapt to expectations. There are sceptics who believe the industry hasn't done enough to address the sustainability issues of both environmental and social concerns.

The UN report of the World Commission on Environment and Development stresses that sustainability is about meeting the needs of the present without compromising the ability of future generations to meet their own needs. In the context of the fashion business, there has an increase in the awareness on such sustainability commitment, especially among the bigger fashion companies. But awareness is not adequate.

Developments

Recent developments include the development of ethical fashion. The Ethical Fashion Forum, which covers a broad range of supply chain activities, will include activities from design and production to retail, inclusion of fair-trade labelling, the practice of sustainable production, and a greater stand on the need to respect the environment and animal welfare. Ethical fashion has now been embraced by hundreds of fashion brands in development, production, and distribution supply chain. This goes beyond apparel to include accessories and footwear.

The United States supermarket chain Walmart has given their support, and the trend will continue to include concern for human and animal rights etc. This indicates that support will continue with the younger consumers. In a recent survey, almost 70 per cent of those surveyed would choose brands that are associated with ethical practices. A 2016 Morgan Stanley research in the United Kingdom found that when it comes to choosing their clothing brands, many would pay attention to the ethical credentials that tells the buyer the source and the material used.

The biggest driver of change in this industry will come from the demand side. If the industry is to go further from just the recycling-and-reuse concept, consumers can play a crucial decider. Choosing an eco-friendly fabric or a ready-made one is not easy as all of these have impact on the environment, let alone its social impacts.

There are already campaigns on labelling. Garments as well as accessories are labelled, informing consumers of what they are purchasing. The Fairtrade mark is probably most recognisable by its logo. To be Fairtrade certified, one must go through a process of meeting Fairtrade standards and being audited by independent global certification body. The Fairtrade standards are aimed at ensuring economic, social, and environmental support for small-scale farmers, which includes prohibition of child labour.

For example, garments with a Fairtrade sticker simply mean the cotton used has been sourced from a Fairtrade-certified producer organisation in a developing country. What it also means is the farmer who produces that will be receiving a fair and stable price for their raw materials. Fairtrade covers well over 1.65 million farmers and more than 1,300 producer certified organisations. There are even standards produced through the World Fair Trade Organization and International Labour Organization.

Despite the advancement made towards ensuring a more sustainable supply chain, it will always be a challenge when it comes to the demand side, where the question will be centred on whether shoppers do care about the environment when they choose their fashion wear or accessories. There are now choices for shoppers to go organic when it comes to choosing materials for their garments. Organic materials cost more but not necessarily less in their carbon footprint. In response to these challenges, recycling is being considered, but it remains to be seen whether it is scalable. Recycling material will place less stress on resources used. Timberland has moved into this recycled space.

It may be impossible to totally prevent cruelty to animals, and neither can the industry rid itself of the environmental and social impacts of its supply chain activities. All of these are not illegal, which makes job of the concerned organisations even more challenging.

As demonstrated by the success of NGOs to persuade fashion companies to stop (and to some extent, they have been successful), it demands more ethical shopping habits, which will be the next battleground for those committed to such a cause.

CHAPTER 11

Sustainable banking

Financial institutions, especially commercial banks, have often been accused of not helping those who really need financial assistance. Banks have been the targets of their critics for the lack of transparency in their decision-making process, and such allegations have not been helpful to their reputation either. Banks' lending and investment policies have also been criticised for supporting large ecological damaging projects, especially in property development, coal fired power plants and plantations that have adverse impact on environment and social consequences.

However, banks often may not see these as lacking in their corporate responsibility. Promoting responsible environmental stewardship and socially responsible development often gets the back seat when it comes to economic viable project development. Hence, they often ignore the fact that in financing such projects, they are indirectly responsible for sound environmental and social management practices. To the banks its strictly their bread and butter.

Championing environmental cause

To an extent, there are global banks taking the application of corporate social responsibility more seriously. Not only are they adopting CSR as the means of managing their corporate risks and reputation, they are committed to treating it as a business process to ensure accountability and transparency. Leading banks are now placing strong emphasis on community sensitivity and taking the green issues more seriously than in the past. HSBC Bank is one example when it made its decision not to support logging business in Sarawak.

The Equator Principles drawn up by ABN AMRO, Barclays, Citibank, and WestLB in collaboration with the World Bank's International Finance Corporation is a prime example, where today in its fifteenth year since its inception, the movement boasts of ninety-four member banks in thirty-seven countries. These member banks share the common objectives of adopting guidelines of the Equator Principles in project finance transactions, especially for emerging markets. There are no more than twelve banks from Asia, one of the fastest-growing regions. None of the larger banks in South-East Asia are members. There is no indication on whether the local banks in this region will ever adopt such bold principles to enhance sustainable development and protect biodiversity.

While there is evidence the financial sector has taken notice of their roles and contributions towards the United Nations' SDGs, there are many others that would prefer their bottom-line priority at the top of their agenda.

Banks as good corporate citizens

The reasons are simply that banks are traditionally big sponsors of philanthropic and sporting activities, community development, education, and donations. A large percentage of local banks, especially those in Asia, consider such social contributions as corporate social responsibility. It is fair to say that such an obligation by giving back to the community forms an important part of their philanthropic and community activities.

Banks can do better

It is obvious there is room for greater integration of the concept and application of sustainability in banks. The adoption of environmental consideration will broaden the role of the banking sector in sustainable development. Today, banks are subjected to demands for transparency and accountability, and it makes a lot of sense to put CSR at the heart of their business strategy to contribute to sustainable business and environment.

The banks' roles towards society and environment will come under the spotlight of scrutiny as awareness of their impacts will gather pace. Some of the best practice in CSR demonstrates the potential of what banks can do to contribute towards environmental and social sustainability.

Increasingly, financial institutions are expected to demonstrate a greater commitment to go beyond corporate governance compliances. Banks will need to take a greater interest in ecology and environment. Protecting the environment forms the core of sustainability development. Ensuring project financing that is environmentally sound should be considered, to minimise reputation risk.

But banks potentially can do more than that; for instance, by integrating environmental and social considerations into their supply chain of product design, to lending policies, banks can play a more influential role towards sustainable development. Attention must be focused on impacts on society and environment as risk, beyond financial and credit risk. Experience of protests, deforestation as a result of land clearing, uprooting rural settlements to make way for hydroelectric projects, and even mining that causes pollution in the community are examples banks must be additionally sensitive when it comes to project financing. Being open to criticism is one thing, but banks risk the call for widespread consumer boycott.

Strengthening of the review procedures on the environmental and social impacts is part of the process and the application of project financing standards. Today, IFC works with several regulators through the Sustainable Banking network. The network is based on tripartite arrangement of member banks that subscribe to Equator Principles, regulators, and IFC. The standards adopted by IFC are in line with its environmental and social sustainability guidelines and the sustainable development goals. Past discussions and developments on projects that were centred on carbon pricing, renewable energy projects and responsible investment that have put society interest above other priorities.

Hard choice

Only time will tell whether the local financial institutions will rise to the challenge and work towards some form of green sustainability. Like everything else, the chief executives will be confronted with the hard choice between making more money and doing their bit towards the country's sustainable development.

Beyond the environmental concern, the global financial crisis of 2008/09 saw the widespread manipulation of the money market rates that resulted in several banks being fined heavily by their regulators. On 30 July 2014, Reuters reported what Bank of England (BOE) Governor Mark Carney wrote to Lloyds Bank chairman Norman Blackwell on the bank's attempted manipulation of the London Inter-bank Offered Rate (LIBOR). The BOE governor Mark Carney was quoted to have said, 'Such manipulation is highly reprehensible, clearly unlawful and may amount to criminal conduct on the part of the individuals involved.'

The GBP218 million in fines on Lloyds come at a time when the industry is seeking answers to massive ethical issues and drastic loss of public trust. Lloyds' joining an unenviable list of global banks guilty of a variety of unacceptable conduct clearly reinforces the authorities' conviction that a major overhaul and installation of the industry ethos and professionalism as the main engine of the industry is an urgent to-do on the agenda.

Case for ethical agenda

Given the context of the sustainability changes to banks in both the Asian and Western markets, there must be concerted efforts in ensuring a common understanding of the changes necessary for them to play a meaningful role in sustainable development.

There are already in place in the more advanced markets a higher standard of ethics, responsibility, and professionalism towards public interest across the local financial services industry. Importantly, its remit is to ensure the convergence and harmonisation of standards of professionalism and ethical behaviours, through the sharing of research, international best practices, and partnership with the industry.

Such development is timely. Banks beyond the advanced markets, especially those in Asia, must embrace and integrate the wider agenda of professional ethics from boardroom to branches, which includes ensuring the code of ethics is well understood across the business mainstream and reminding staff to fulfil their continuing professional development obligations, including business and professional ethics.

Higher standards of professionalism

The Standards of Professional Conduct will not only demand a set of well-defined behavioural standards on professionalism and integrity; they are expected to comply with laws and regulations, and exercise independence and objectivity. In this regulated sector, members are prohibited from insider trading, tipping, and market manipulation. Members must also exercise duties of fairness and objectivity and observe strictly client confidentiality. Professional conduct includes rules on members' duties in observing loyalty to their employers, and avoidance of potential conflict of interest. Indeed, any potential conflicts of interest must be disclosed openly and fairly. As in the case of good practices of professional bodies, members will not be allowed to engage in activities that may potentially harm the reputation and integrity of the institute, including misrepresentation.

Wider agenda

Banks would already have in place a robust framework including code of ethics. The real challenge is demonstrating and walking values of ethics and professionalism in its business mainstream. In this context, it is necessary for banks to ensure public interests are protected through professional conduct and actions reflecting the values that the banks espouse.

There is now even a Global Alliance for Banking on Values (GABV), a network of member banks from all over the world. GABV, founded in 2009, is committed to advance the concept of social, environmental, and business sustainability. The alliance of banks gets together regularly to share and promote a sustainable financial future by collaborating in projects that add value to a sustainable future.

To achieve such wider agenda, professional conduct remains an integral part of governance role, where moral values and behaviours are well demonstrated, supported, and recognised. Policy regulators are fully aware that cultures, values, and behaviours will require a wider stakeholder engagement. This comes with cooperation and assistance from businesses that are prepared to walk the values of ethics and professionalism.

The key challenge here is to ensure the standards and ethical behaviours are being observed in delivering mainstream banking so that these will influence the way banks behave. It is a real test for the global banks.

CHAPTER 12

Socially responsible investment

Socially responsible investment, or most commonly known as SRI for short, is also called green investment in advanced markets; elsewhere, terms such as *ethical investment* or *social investment* are being used. All of these have one common purpose, i.e. an investment with a deliberate aim to bring about social or environmental change.

Pioneers

Socially responsible investment is not a new concept. Business historians will recall the Quakers pioneered responsible investment during the seventeenth century. Accordingly, Natural Investment LLC, in one of their articles, mentioned that the Quakers advocated social justice, from slavery to women's rights, prison reform, and armament issues. The article recalled that *as early as 1688, Quaker meetings in the United States were already discussing the ethical issue of profiting from the slave trade, and in 1758, the Philadelphia*

*yearly meeting unanimously issued a proclamation forbidding
its members from participating in the slave trade.*

This shaped the investment policy; till today, the
Quakers have a total of five principles which derived from
their spiritual thinking—truth and integrity, justice, equality
and community, simplicity, peace and the earth and the
environment. Based on these principles, the Quakers'
investment of their members' savings excludes sectors
that have elements of pornography, prostitution, arms and
munitions, and fossil-fuel extraction. Quakers' investment
portfolios generally have public interest in mind, and as such,
sectors like tobacco, alcohol, and gambling are restricted to
no more than 5 per cent of total portfolio.

Past trends show that socially responsible investment
trends became more pronounced and recognised as a potential
force to drive social agenda and issues, including civil rights
in the sixties and seventies. The global campaign against
apartheid in South Africa, for example, included pressure on
foreign investors to withdraw their investment from the country.
This has not only raised public awareness on important social
issues but also questioned the social responsibility of business
and, importantly, their corporate image and reputation.

Since then, the concept of socially responsible investment
continues to evolve as demands from society have moved
rapidly from raising awareness to taking real actions. Body
Shop was one of the early brands that embraced a no-animal-
testing commitment; the company rapidly expanded into a
global enterprise that generates revenue worth USD1.4 billion.

Wider coverage

Today the definition of socially responsible investment
is wider, but it has more definitive scope on what it means to

be socially responsible. The definition of socially responsible includes the promotion of environmental protection, public interest, gender equality, human rights, consumer protection, and health issues. The definition even extends to those perceived to lead to negative social elements. These include tobacco, gambling, and arms.

There are now newer areas classified under the broad term of responsible investing, summarised under the heading of environmental, social, and governance (ESG) issues: environment, social justice, and corporate governance. These are nicknamed 'invest good' and are applied as a basis by ethical fund managers to invest and build portfolios. Indeed, in many instances, past cases of bribery, corruption, and fraud convinced the fund managers of the need to invest in such good business. In many instances, all these fund managers are assisted by their research guided by processes including proactive practices such as overall objectives, values of impact on both community and shareholder.

Such basis is used for example in the case of MSCI ESG research, where they apply three common principles of integration, values, and impact. Ethical considerations based on defined principles and alignment with values are significant towards investment decision. The ESG factors are used in the investment decision process alongside financial analysis of the portfolio. The environmental considerations, for example, look into carbon emissions and footprint. Fast forward, a global issue such as climate change vulnerability is now an important but real consideration.

Managing risks

An integral part of this process is the fact that investors are looking at the risk perspective of the sustainability challenges, including volatile weather patterns that will influence food security, and even demographic shifts. As investors continue to re-evaluate their position, the traditional investment approach is no longer adequate as risk factors include unpredictability of weather, and uncertainty in social stability. All of these have led to further perspectives of investors. Today, there are more than 1,500 institutional investors that are signatories to the United Nations Principles for Responsible Investing. There are equally many more that are committed to embrace the principles of the UN Sustainable Development Goals.

An important segment of ESG is community investing. This important push towards this direction can be found in the 1980s, when most would recall the Bhopal and Exxon *Valdez* environmental disasters that questioned credibility and trust of the multinationals involved. Issues involving workers interest also questioned the licence to operate of Nike in Indonesia, Shell in Nigeria, and more recently, BP off the Gulf of Mexico. All of these did attract fund managers' attention.

The global financial crisis of 2008/09 also provided a stark reminder of the interdependence between societies, economies, and financial markets. The financial crisis nearly brought the world to its knees, and it indirectly impacted on the confidence level of investors but did re-emphasise the role of investors, as long-term owners of companies, to ensure good stewardship and public trust. It also provided clear evidence that market pressures do not always result in ideal outcomes for the wider public good.

Increased regulation and pressure from the millennial generation, those most affected by the fallout of the financial crisis, has reinforced the involvement of corporations with the society in which they operate, and the duties they have to all stakeholders.

Financial capital is being used to enable access for the poor to capital to help with small business, enabling regeneration of communities in the inner cities. The aim is to finance initiatives to help the poor and the underserved communities. The Nobel Peace Prize winner Muhammad Yunus gave finance a rethink of their lending practice by inventing microfinance for the poor segment of society. Grameen Bank became a model for microfinance, and it was emulated across many emerging markets. In many ways, microfinance went on to become a means to assist in promoting social sustainability activities, especially in less-developed countries.

The concept of social sustainability involves a wide range of health, education, and social welfare issues. Financing of such sustainable investing also takes into consideration how labour is being treated; that ranges from workplace health and safety to human capital development. It is within such contexts that businesses invest in concerns to eradicate tropical diseases, AIDS, even access to clean water.

Such strategy involves typically both private firms and publicly listed companies; the shareholder engagement and governance are being watched carefully. Sustainable investing strategies work together to encourage a responsible board that will demand appropriate corporate behaviours and image.

Institutional investors will want to invest their mutual funds that specialise in seeking companies with sound and string reputation in compliance, transparency, and accountability.

Investors of sustainable investment typically comprise of pension fund, community development funds that have a specific mission of serving funds that have high-social-impact investments in line with their missions.

Growing trends

Today, the value of socially responsible investment funds is worth in their billions. According to the MSCI Blog, nearly USD31 trillion in assets under management were invested in funds that consider ESG issues in their investing process as of January 2018; this represents a 34 per cent increase from two years previously. It is believed such investment funds have almost tripled from USD206 billion to USD588 billion, and the number of funds increased 89 per cent from 413 to 780.

Global fund managers such as MSCI believe a new generation of investors, the millennial generation, has already emerged. Valued at between USD15 and 20 trillion across the ESG investment portfolio, this is almost double that of US equity market.

Sustainable and responsible investing spans a wide and growing range of products and asset classes, embracing not only public equity investments (stocks), but also cash, fixed income and alternative investments, such as private equity, venture capital, and real estate. SRI investors, like conventional investors, seek a competitive financial return on their investments. Elsewhere, fund managers are witnessing responsible investment gaining ground in China, one of the largest economies in the world. Many justifiably believe that concept of environmental, social, and governance investments are gaining acceptance because of interest in renewable energy technologies resulting from support from both government and boardroom commitment.

Asset managers reported that the concept of ESG investment in China is already being widely embraced by companies and investors because of favourable Chinese policies that are pushing towards green finance developments, and such positive confidence is justifiable by the fact China is fast becoming a producer of electric cars, and owns the world's largest network of electric public transport. China is committed to reducing its fair share of carbon emission, and its government has introduced and enforced stricter regulation to protect the environment. Through its Belt and Road Initiative, China has planned for massive investment in green infrastructures covering its energy, transport, and agriculture sectors.

Another sign of China getting more serious with a more sustainable development is the new requirement from the China Securities Regulatory Commission that by the year 2020, all listed companies and bond issuers would need to disclose their ESG risks in their operations. The Shanghai and Shenzhen stock exchanges are reported to have committed to supporting the development of green and transparent markets in China by supporting the UN Sustainable Stock Exchanges initiative.

Low-carbon economies

The upward growth in sustainable investment is expected to grow in line with the growing transition of many markets moving towards low-carbon economies. Rising global temperatures have led to melting of the Arctic ice sheets and possible increase in the sea levels; all of these represent massive risk to humankind in the next century.

Mitigating measures, especially in renewable energy projects, environmental management, and recycling plants, represent fresh opportunities, and all of these require massive funding. The resulting consequence has also been proliferation of new funding mechanisms, including crowdfunding, venture capital and private equity funds, and privately arranged hedge funds. This has resulted in massive growth in social community investment, and according to MSCI, over the last decade, the related fund has nearly doubling in assets between 2014 and 2016 and growing just over 50 per cent from 2016 to 2018.

Performance

There have been several studies on correlation between social investment and their sound returns. Studies conducted by Oxford University, Deutsche Asset & Wealth Management, Morgan Stanley Institute for Sustainable Investing found majority of funds of ESG standards to be positive in financial performance.

CNBC reported on 13 May 2019 that there are now more than USD12 trillion worth of social investment funds, and that is easily one of four of the total assets managed in the United States. There is also a growing trend among companies to produce a sustainability report. All of these point to the fact that socially responsible investing trend is not a fad, but here to stay.

The challenge of climate change isn't going to go away tomorrow; while socially responsible investment continues to go into the mainstream, change in investment strategies will now consider not only fundamentals but also ESG data analytics, and those who can do well in this will most likely succeed with their investment portfolios. The *Financial Times*, on 18 September 2018, published an article reiterating the positive financial returns from ESG, based on more than 2,000 academic research studies over the past forty years. The same report also indicated that socially responsible funds had an annualised return of more than 10 per cent.

Within this context, it is important to note that ethical leadership in the development of socially responsible investment will be more meaningful to any positive outcome, especially faced with pressures and competition from the investment community. It is easier to fall into the temptation of more traditional investment that may have higher financial returns and predictability.

It is more so, then, that ethical leadership is needed as the whole basis on why socially responsible investment is necessary, i.e. to plan for the future of a better place, and in doing so, a safer and healthier global community at large. It is above all the right thing to do, as David Wallace-Wells concluded in his book *The Uninhabitable Earth*, '*you can't choose the planet which is the one any of us call home.*'

CHAPTER 13

Jobs, roles, and skills in the digital age

The fourth industrial revolution has arrived. The world around us has changed. Many grew up during the industrial age, which saw wealth and convenience grow exponentially.

The world has now entered the digital age, where so much has been written and talked about on impacts of artificial intelligence and robotics, the Internet of Things, biotechnology, and so on that McKinsey Global Institute is predicting that one area which is most impacted is work and organisations.

Business context

Digital impacts on infrastructures and delivery systems have brought about massive changes within both public and private sectors. Business transformation of this nature has brought higher efficiencies and conveniences through improved processes and opportunities. Even in the deployment of technology, for example, through the Internet of Things

(IoT), there is higher integration of physical devices through applications to enable economic and social benefits. Evidently, we now see higher extension of Internet connectivity to drive a variety of standard devices from desktops to smartphones to support both business and social lifestyles.

It is expected that as much as 60 per cent of present work tasks and activities worldwide are likely to be displaced by 2030. Majority of these would be the automation of work tasks involving what is commonly known as semiskilled and unskilled jobs.

Indeed, such a prediction is in line with the World Economic Forum's 'The Future of Jobs' report that by the year 2022, no less than 54 per cent of all employees will require significant reskilling and upskilling.

Forces

Many experts would agree that it is hard to ignore the disruptions technology has brought about to business processes and experiences. This has impacted on the future design of work. Lessons from business history show that while technology has always played a key role towards shaping work, it has also created new and future work opportunities that do not exist today. For example, we need to go no further than the digital revolution to witness how it has transformed the way we communicate and connect to each other without borders and 24/7.

From a sustainability perspective, technological changes will continue to transform and improve the nature of work and services. The digital transformation of business offers immense opportunities to help support the culture of sustainability. The sustainability challenges from impacts of climate change to access and affordability are not going away so easily, and some studies have shown digital initiatives involve the adoption of energy efficiency technology, will help as mitigating measures. Progression to a more sustainable economy involving digital and technology innovations offer new job opportunities from data analysis to production of biodegradables.

The European Commission sees the arrival of the digital economy as the opportunity to promote greater inclusive growth, at the same time fostering conditions that will enable creation of jobs in a more sustainable manner. These include new a sustainability enterprise in more environmentally friendly products and services that are e-enabled, and one that will involve training to raise digital literacy. Policies are being crafted to support a much more inclusive growth as part of their commitment to social sustainability.

The increasing popularity of the gig economy has given rise to greater job autonomy and control accelerated by new technology applications. AirBNB and Uber are well known examples of the collaborative economy that allows sharing of jobs, and flexibility to individuals who prefer part-time roles or a variety of jobs to spend their time.

In her book *The Future of Work Is Already Here*, Professor Lynda Gratton at the London Business School predicted five prevailing forces that would shape the future of work. It is no surprise that among these main forces, she identified the force of energy resources. The ever-rising cost of energy and the threat of climate change are offering fresh opportunities for new employment while at the same time, eliminating the ones that have contributed to rise in greenhouse gas emissions.

Technology has always been one of the main drivers behind the economic advancement of many nations. Societal changes and improvements are just one of the many possibilities of such scientific advancement. Professor Gratton identified these forces

1. Rising technology capability and connectivity between five billion people,
2. The opportunity offered through cloud computing,
3. Continuous productivity and social participation,
4. Digitalisation of knowledge, and use of energy resources,
5. Replacement of traditional jobs.

These forces have shaped the world, as we know. The world has experienced the pervasiveness of digital technology in both our work and private homes. It is within such a context that many experts do expect to witness the continuing changes to roles, jobs, and people.

Broad perspectives

These impacts can be narrowed into several different perspectives that will shape the future of how organisations and individuals manage the transition.

Jobs

There are hardly any jobs that are not impacted by technology disruption. The past three decades saw the rise in productivity because of technology. There was a phenomenal rise in the number of transactional businesses that have been automated. It is not just in assembly line but also services across all industries.

The number of new jobs created from such phenomenal changes can be seen from mushrooming of new jobs, from big data analysis to on-line marketing and services. From the introduction of IBM's mainframe to the use of tablets, in these forty years, employees have greatly benefitted from additional convenience, speed and services across every sector. In many ways, the risk of health and safety hazards has also been eliminated through automation of certain tasks through technology. Hence, we need to recognise that automation is impacting on tasks and not jobs. Automation through new technology has also helped to drive scalability, and such organisational effectiveness wouldn't have been possible in the days of manual and routine duties.

In under one decade, business and society have also benefitted from improvement to production, right down to improvement in lifestyle of individuals. Technology advancement has also improved medical fields, where not only exposure to hazards is lessened, but also medical specialists and doctors are now in a better position to diagnose their patients with greater precision and importantly saving lives.

Fast forward to today, we are into advanced technology where the IoT allows us to connect to just about anything through physical devices. Through our mobile phones and laptops, we communicate better, shop, play and even interface with whoever we want, anywhere, 24/7. The Economist newspaper in its September 14th 2019, issue wrote that the IOT aims to do for information what electricity did for energy. The IOT has been a slow revolution, as it will transform the way in just about anything changing the world in its process, one forecast it reported that by 2035 the world will have a trillion connected computers from food packaging to the consumer wear.

Organisational roles

From the organisational perspective, today's digital environment has increased the opportunity to introduce and allow greater innovation, and autonomy to decision-making. An example is the connected culture, which demands greater teamwork and cooperation, and greater emphasis on the gathering, analysis, and storage of information intelligence.

Skills

The ability to analyse and adapt to faster and unpredictable environments is perhaps an emerging competency that will be the differentiator. There will be conscious shift towards depth rather than width. Mastery of skills, on the other hand, the trend is towards greater specialisation, as emphasis is on what you know. All these mean everyone must have the ability to leverage on technology solutions as well as industry trends and experiences to drive their own experiences. Moreover in a sustainable world, there will be unlimited opportunities to embrace such skills and development.

Another wave of change to jobs and roles will witness a broader but horizontal career road map, where multitasking and coordination skills in a networked environment will be necessary. There is then the need to revisit the whole concept of career development. The digital era will likely mark the end of lifetime employment, and vertical management progression will come to an end. Indeed, career routes will be less structured, and collaborative. In a new artificial-intelligence era, growth in the gig economy will accelerate, which will see more outsourcing and thus more employees on short-term contracts with flexible locations and hours. In terms of functional changes, there will be a constant shift from functional hierarchy to a network-based organisation, which will not only de-emphasise titles but also re-emphasise skills and capabilities, and these continue to evolve as the digital age demands more fluidity and responsiveness.

Digital

In the digital age, skill acquisition will become more participative, as knowledge becomes more digitised and more important. There will be the greater use of IOT with all hundreds if not thousands of mobile applications that provide flexibility to working adults to pursue any continuous learning. The upskilling or training purpose has already manifested in the proliferation of fast-growing digital education companies providing online tuition. A recent Babson Survey Research Group even suggests that 6.7 million post-secondary students are taking at least one online course, compared to just 1.6 million in 2001. However, for online learning to be available, access to Internet is a must, and given the inadequacy of digital infrastructure in remote parts of some countries, access remains a challenge. Equally important is the adaptability of learning styles towards online, as learning in isolation may not be practical for a working adult. There is a general agreement that e-learning technologies will continue to evolve and become much more accessible and interactive through mobile devices, empowering the younger workforce to construct their own meaning and digital identity.

With greater emphasis on sustainability footprint, the digital economy will see growth of more technical specialisation. Regardless of the shape of technology, inputs will come heavily from sciences. Technology has contributed to improvement in use of research across all sciences. For example, progress in life sciences will experience more leaps and bounds, as demand for better health care and treatment grows. The advancement made by the sciences has made artificial intelligence more impactful; as such, we will see greater integration into development of driverless cars, and even use of robotics across all economic sectors.

Managing the digital economy means that performance management will have to be more agile and responsive. Organisations may have to consider discarding the old concept of the 'bell curve' approach in favour of new models that give greater weight on short-term and intangible contributions. In the digital age, the shift from muscle power to more brainpower is complex and more stressful. Thinking tasks will see the inclusion of indirect contribution in future reward culture. This requires a different concept of how expectations are established, conversed, and accepted. As teamwork demands greater collaboration, so too is the need to place priorities on inclusion and diversity management. Reward practices will be focused on individual competencies and less dependent on a structured pay system.

The digital economy is expected to bring about drastic change in the way jobs are being designed, roles being managed, and skills being developed. But all these in a virtual world will require support and understanding for many individuals to navigate successfully through the changes. Empathy as well as mentoring skills will hence become handy. The future of work will demand individuals to be empowered and agile and responsive to change. As we move from a more functional and controlled environment to one that is that is more flexible and responsive, there is no denying that challenges are bound to be plentiful.

CHAPTER 14

Sustainability and the Olympics

The Tokyo Olympics 2020 promises to go green. It is consistent with the International Olympic Committee (IOC) commitment to sustainability.

The IOC knows that for each modern Olympics, the games leave behind a bigger carbon footprint, which critics have rightly questioned, especially over the IOC's commitment to make the Olympics go green. In response, one IOC member, Mario Pescante, was quoted to have said at a Global Engagement and Empowerment Forum that the IOC remained committed to embracing sustainability principles and practices in every single aspect of the games, more so in the 2020 Tokyo summer games.

Tokyo commitment to zero carbon

In the world where reducing carbon emissions has become a must-do agenda, the Tokyo organising committee is fully committed to work towards zero carbon during the preparations and throughout the games. For example, the organisers intend to use renewable energy from solar and wind to power the games stadiums. Importantly, the Games Village and the public transport will utilise low-energy technology and recycled materials and fuel cell buses respectively. Interestingly, Tokyo promises to accelerate recycling wherever possible, and one example is to recycle old mobile phones into 5,000 medals. The use of technology will apply artificial intelligence, using robotics to serve and ensure minimal greenhouse gas emissions and energy consumption.

These development plans reflect Japan's status as a serious economic powerhouse committed to build low-carbon Olympics. According to the World Economic Forum report, Japan, with a gross national output worth US$850 billion, is focusing on environmental sustainability. Japan imports 100 per cent of its oil and gas and reducing its carbon footprint is an important policy initiative for the future. Beyond this, Tokyo is determined to make the 2020 Olympics a true example of the future—sustainable and carbon neutral.

Sustainability activities

The IOC supports the United Nations Sustainable Development Goals. Its sustainability strategy has a total of eighteen broad objectives across infrastructure, sourcing, and resourcing management, including its mobility, workforce, and energy usage. In line with this, the Tokyo Olympics will embed every aspect of the sustainability goals in their activities, delivery, and outcomes. Some of the key supporting activities in line with the sustainability framework and strategy are as follows:

1.   The Tokyo Olympics organisers have in place process that will ensure respect for the human rights of all people

involved in the preparation and delivery of the Games,
A number of fora to raise awareness and awareness-
building activities focusing on respect for human
rights, diversity, and gender have been initiated. The
Tokyo 2020 organisers have also put in place internal
development exercise to support diversity and inclusion
among its own staff and external stakeholders.

2. The Tokyo 2020 medal project is in place to
   spearhead the production of the 5,000 Games medals
   from recycled materials, primarily discarded mobile
   phones. It was reported that by the end of 2018, close
   to fifty thousand tons of discarded devices and an
   astonishing five million used mobile phones had
   been collected from various centres in the country.
   Local governments supported this project, including
   the use of wood for improving public utilities;

3. The adherence to international standards from
   procurement to hiring ensures the organisers are
   adopting rules and international standards in
   their operations and practices. One example is the
   adoption of Sustainable Sourcing Code so that all
   sourcing and purchasing of materials meet the ethical
   code of practice;

4. Responsible practices towards third-party hiring are
   put in place, and useful fora between relevant parties
   have taken place, ensuring clarity of purpose and
   standards;

5. Energy-saving measures are given priorities at
   most places, and renewable energy technology has
   been a criterion in determining the type of energy,
   including use of solar energy cells being installed on
   the roads leading to the stadiums. The carbon-offset
   programme is already in place.

To reinforce Tokyo's commitments towards sustainability goals for the 2020 summer games, the guiding principles read, 'Be better, together—for the planet and the planet.' Its commitments towards the United Nations Sustainable Goals are well spelled out in its sustainability themes.

1. Climate change
2. Natural environment and biodiversity
3. Resource management
4. Consideration of human rights
5. Labour and fair business practices

Although much effort has gone into ensuring the sustainability themes are well entrenched in the activities leading to the summer games of 2020, the economic and social impacts of the Olympics are hard to miss. Past experiences have shown not only huge carbon footprint from greenhouse gas emissions; the costs can very substantial. Experiences from Rio de Janeiro's hosting of the Olympics Summer Games in 2016 showed almost an environmental disaster as well as leaving the country heavily in financial debt.

Rio missed carbon footprint target

According to a case study by Sylvia Trendafilova, Jeffrey Graham, and James Bemiller, 'Sustainability and the Olympics: The case of the 2016 Rio Summer Games', Rio ended with a huge environmental footprint. The joint case study printed in the *Journal of Sustainability Education* of 14 January 2018 gave some startling figures on carbon footprint! Flying an estimated 28,500 athletes and staff to Brazil for the 2016 Summer Olympics in Rio generated more than 2,000 kilotonnes (kt) of greenhouse gases (GHGs)—not to mention the 2,500 kt of GHGs associated with bringing in about half a million spectators.

Additionally, Rio struggled with demands of additional infrastructures to ensure clean water, proper sanitation, and environment. What's even more disappointing to the non-governmental organisations is the amount of financial debt the city has got into, where many facilities became white elephants. Rio is perhaps not a fair comparison to, say, London in 2012, which won gold in the Environmental and Sustainability category of the 6th International Sports Event Management Awards. London won the greenest games to date; the organisers did manage to reduce its energy consumption by 20 per cent, although it did not quite live up to the target of renewable energy utilisation.

Environmental and social challenges

In comparison, the Rio economy was experiencing an economic recession, and governance responsibilities were not as strong as once thought. There were also delays resulting in project overruns, and poor management also led to water contamination. Even on the social front, the shifting of inner-city squatters to make way for a new Olympic Park could have been managed much better. All of these have called into question the ability of the Games organisers, and the failure to assure its sceptics.

The Olympics are never short of criticisms. Once accused of lack of transparency and questionable selection process of the host city, not one host has exceeded the goals and targets. There are more criticisms than praises on the way the Olympics were managed and, more importantly, its economic, social, and environmental impacts on the city and its surroundings.

Hosting the Olympic Games has become a big industry. The cost has gone into billions of US dollars. Each time, the successful city which bid for the rights must spend easily billions on construction of huge stadiums, facilities, roads, Olympic Village, hotels, etc. There is always a risk that some of these facilities will become white elephants, as in the case of Athens in 2004, where a number of their facilities were left to a state of disrepair. Similarly in Rio, because of cost of maintenance, a number of games facilities were left unattended.

Raising of sustainability bar

The IOC has made sustainable development a must-have in every aspect of what the city has to do. Not every city has resources deep enough to fulfil every single criterion of going carbon neural.

Nonetheless, sustainable development is now a necessary success factor. On the brighter side, such a stretched target would be good to follow, as the preparations allow the city to do an urban renewal as in the case of London or even an opportunity to put in place much-needed transport infrastructure in the case of Rio.

With each Olympics, the sustainability bar is being raised. That's partly because of the availability of green technology and much better acceptance of the city and its immediate stakeholders' support.

With better guidelines and capacity, there is no reason why Tokyo should not do one better.

CHAPTER 15

Sustainability and cities

Cities are where most of the major economic activities and actions take place. The urban convenience and amenities are not only attractions to economic migrants in search of hope and opportunities, but computers from food packaging to. These reasons explain the cause of rural urban migration a trend which most economists would identify as reasons for urbanisation growth and challenges.

Economic opportunities have for decades lifted millions out of their poverty traps, and to most of them, provided them the security of home and income stability over several generations. Such economic opportunities are pull factors behind international migration taking place in Europe in recent years.

According to Global Data of the world's 35 megacities in 2017, 21 are in Asia and it is estimated that 60% of future megacities will be in the Asian continent by 2025 including 11 already in China and 6 in India. The largest inhabitants will be in the metropolitans of Shanghai, Jakarta and Tokyo each having more than 30 million population.

Among Asia's most crowded cities especially the several mega cities of China, India and Pakistan are now home to another 1.1 billion people over the next two decades as the poor especially from rural parts of the country continue to be drawn to the relatively better economic and social opportunities offered in the cities.

However, not all will find such urban advantage to be easily accessible and affordable. The United Nations studies shows that approximately 700 million people live in urban slum. Majority are struggling to cope with the environmental degradation, access to clean water, waste disposal and lacking basic sanitation services – all these a result of gradual rise in demand from growing urban population over time. It is well documented that pollution, and hygienic conditions pose threat to potential health epidemics, and rising urban slums are already reaching at critical and alarming levels.

Maintaining economic growth yet giving urban population decent housing and access to basic services are biggest challenges facing any urban planners especially in emerging Asian cities. According to United Nations, by 2030, 59 percent of the world's population, or 5 billion will live and work in cities. Such prediction means urban planners who will need to consider among the priorities are infrastructure support that includes access to clean and safe water, electricity, waste and sanitation and importantly a transport system for masses.

The McKinsey studies show that cities are generators of economic growth, and thereby responsible for easily 70 percent of carbon emissions. Despite the huge amount of wealth generated from the cities, contributing at least 80% of any national GDP, there are many economic and social issues associated generally with urban cities. Not only many are deprived of basic urban services and housing, many urban dwellers face potential crimes, pollutions, health issues and stability. Urban pollution for example remains a constant problem across many regions. Air pollution contributes towards the emission of greenhouse gases.

Sustainable Development Goals (SDGs) for Cities

The United Nations Environment considers such environmental and social concerns as part of the sustainability development ambition that they intend to encourage by adopting a more sustainable consumption and production practice model in over-populated Asia region, as an example. This is in line with the one of the sustainable development goals (SDG) on cities i.e. SDG 11 (sustainable cities and human settlements).

The SDG 11 focuses on ensuring access to housing and basic services, sustainable transport system, sustainable urbanization, access to public spaces, sustainable buildings, per capita environmental impact of cities, and policies towards climate change, resource efficiency and disaster risk reduction. All these triple concerns of economic, environmental and social issues are significant as these are very related to the national economic and social agenda of any city planners.

Working in partnerships

Close alliance between governments, businesses and non- governmental organisations are necessary to achieve the targets of a better environmental and socially acceptable lifestyles that include recycling and green businesses focusing on green technologies and environmental services are opportunities. The public-private-partnerships can work if given the right mechanisms, investment and commitment from government especially towards a proper governance framework, guidance and urban environmental management.

What's a sustainable city

A sustainable city is roughly defined as one that is designed or re-designed with priorities and consideration given to use of renewable energy and less on fossil fuel, clean lifestyle with use of mass transport even driven by electricity and minimal use of energy for warmth, cooling of houses. In the sustainable world, many homes are built to be energy efficient built with environment friendly materials.

The so-called "Green Building" is one aspect of sustainable development. Development experts will not disagree that green building is an essential part towards sustainability since homes are consumers of energy. Good examples are those homes in temperate climate that will need to have boilers to heat the homes, and insulation to keep the heat in. In colder houses make up easily 10% of total energy consumption. In warmer tropical countries, it is common to find homes and offices using the air conditioners to cool the buildings.

The process of building homes does contribute to carbon emission from beginning to end. Unlike the past where energy efficiency is not given the attention. Today, construction of homes would be paid more attention especially towards their use of energy including the type of building material. Others include transportation, pollution from construction activities, use of technology etc constitute important elements towards the development of more sustainable buildings. The economic and social implications from building sector have far reaching implications towards the development of sustainable cities.

The strategic intent of all town planners to ensure their cities are eco- friendly that contain habitats designed towards recycling and use of renewable energy across its social and economic activities.

Ideally, a sustainable city is dependent on the triple pillars of sustainability covering ecology, economics, and society. This is a tough test as any sustainable city must demonstrate its switch to renewable source of energy to power the city's daily activities, and in some places its reliance on its ability to turn trash into energy. In terms of social element, a sustainable city further must embrace the well-respected for diversity, well- connected and generally good governance. A small ecological footprint is always the biggest challenge. There will also be other challenges for many cities to qualify for such high standards, and one which will require matured political system and commitment towards enforcement of rules especially those pertaining to enforcement of governance rules on planning, development as well as educating its citizens on social and environment developments.

Sustainable cities

Despite of the environmental challenges Copenhagen is ranked today as the greenest cities in the world. It became the first city to achieve the status of carbon neutral city. Despite of the cold weather for most of the year, Copenhagen succeeded in achieving an energy efficient system that cut down on waste and improve the carbon emission. The city has also succeeded in building a city transport system that has led to almost 50% of its residents cycling to work!

Stockholm was awarded and recognised as the first European Green Capital by the European Commission back in 2010. The city has successfully blended the environmental element well into the back engine of the city. Examples include real evidence of the city success in driving energy efficiency towards heating and cooling systems of the buildings in the city, put in place an integrated waste system, combating noise pollution, and getting people support towards a more environmentally friendly lifestyle. All of these have led to the city successfully reduced its carbon emissions by 25% per citizen and clearly on its way towards achieving fossil fuel city by year 2050.

Challenges

The two 'sustainable cities' of Copenhagen and Stockholm are exemplary examples, but these are exception rather than norms. From Rio de Janeiro to Beijing, cities across the globe today face overcrowding, and challenges of growing carbon footprint. Aside from climate change challenges, many cities are saddled with inefficiency across its support infrastructures made worse by poor governance and corruption among local government officials.

Urban regeneration seen in older cities have improved their energy efficiency through better technology and system design. But modernising of infrastructures will be necessary for transportation, water management and sanitary and waste controls. The city state of Singapore is one example of a city state doing just that. In its Sustainable Development Blueprint it outlines its sustainability goals 2030, defining its targets of ensuring all its buildings are certified green, a target of achieving energy efficiency by at least 30 per cent and that public transport being made accessible of a 10 minute walk to nearest train station for at least 80 per cent of population.

All these infrastructures require public funding. While several cities have privatised the public services including water and waste management, many cities are still grappling with the problems of bad governance and corruption. In response, several cities have sought external funding from abroad. Jakarta is one example. Home to 10 million people, Jakarta is infamous for traffic crawls, and inner-city problems of inadequate housing and access to water. The recently elected government recently revealed budget of almost 40 trillion US dollars to fund an integrated inner city rail, and rebuild inner city settlements and improve water and waste management – all of these are part of sustainability plan being discussed at a roundtable discussion on Sustainable Cities: Challenges and Opportunities in Jakarta back in 2015.

Sustainability issues remain one of the biggest challenges to overcome in urban planning and development. It is no surprise that big cities share common issues on energy efficiency, infrastructure capacity and policy governance. There is no shortage of good practices where cities can explore, and to rethink of their policy in order to adapt to suit their needs and over- coming the challenges. One thing that no one disputes is that commitment to sustainable development goals is necessary if the cities are to overcome today's overcrowded problems to one that is designed in order to be fit for the future.

CHAPTER 16

Affordable housing

Affordable housing has become a fundamental human need and increasingly a human right across the world. But there is simply not enough to satisfy the ever-growing appetite for affordable homes. The problem is worsened by unplanned urbanisation and shortage of development land to meet growing urban population. These have led to unprecedented growth of inner-city slums, made worse by persistent shortage of affordable housing, especially for new urban poor. Conflict between objectives of urban planners and private landowners has not made it easier for all stakeholders, especially local governments.

Sustainable development goal

There is a now an urgent need to ensure a sustainable future by providing adequate housing for growing cities. There is no magic formula, but governments agree and subscribe to Sustainable Development Goal 11, which is really to *make cities and human settlements inclusive, safe, resilient, and sustainable.*

There are millions of households now in desperate need of a proper roof over their head. A United Nations report on housing needs predicted that six out of ten people will live in urban areas by 2030. Much of this growth is expected to take place in the emerging markets of Asia, Africa, and Latin America. In Asia alone, the United Nations expect that such urbanisation trend will reach a staggering 64 per cent by 2050.

By the same token, by 2050, the world's current population of seven billion will double in size, making it even more demanding and urgent to make housing more affordable and sustainable. Such sustainability challenges will pose challenges to governments to add housing and infrastructure as basic requirements along the same line as food security, health, education, employment opportunities, and public safety.

Today, urban Asia is home to more than 2.0 billion urban dwellers, unmatched by other regions in the world. The United Nations report predicted the number of urban residents in Asia is expected to reach 3.3 billion by 2050. Based on the Asian Development Bank publication *Housing Challenge in Emerging Asia—Options and Solutions*, there is a desperate need for adequate yet affordable housing throughout the region.

Housing crisis

Past decades have witnessed phenomenal growth in the Asian economies, which has led to the inevitable expansion of urban cities. Growing prosperity comes with a growth in the number of middle-class dwellers. This has fuelled the demand for all sorts of services, from new consumers. The increase in demand for housing has also pushed house prices up, often beyond the reach of the locals. Homes have not only become expensive; there are thousands experiencing more expensive financing, and many are forced to live further away from their workplaces.

For those who are less fortunate and earning less, it's the same stories all over. Many of the low-income groups will simply end up in the cheaper and more affordable home in the inner cities, where sanitation and living conditions can be inadequate.

Both regulators and business have no dispute over the urgency to provide decent and adequate housing to millions of households. Indeed, there is an acceptance of such purpose. Guaranteeing a sustainable future for cities remains the vision of all city mayors; however, to realise such a mission, there is now a call for fresh thinking towards such goals. To realise the mission, governments must think innovatively about inclusive approaches to providing housing and addressing the challenges of affordability. The fact that much of the demand comes from poorer segments of the society makes it more necessary to ensure policies are inclusive and sustainable.

The severe lack of affordable housing risks many cities creating ghettos and exclusion zones for the deprived ones. The sustainable development principles have implicitly emphasised the importance of inclusivity, one aspect of which is housing.

There must be new approaches towards funding and bringing the different institutions together. It is in everyone's interest that city development must deliver inclusivity and opportunities, allowing better access. In most of the cases, the need for affordable housing affects easily the bottom 40 per cent of the earners in a country.

Singapore

Singapore has one of the best examples in providing affordable homes for their people. As one of the most densely populated city-states, its government policies towards providing affordable homes started some sixty years ago. Today, its home ownership programme through its Housing Development Board has built more than one million homes, allowing 80 per cent of the population access to homes which they could not afford in the first place. Today the city-state is free of any inner-city slums typically seen in most major cities.

Today, many governments are encouraging all sorts of innovative and more inclusive financing methods. It is never an easy task, as such agenda entails the participation of many stakeholders, many with differing agendas. But a simple approach is about creating a more sustainable community living with access to food, education, public transport, and amenities. Fiscal incentives allowed by the government are often common practice, which means a more inclusive approach is necessary to make housing more affordable.

In the final analysis, there is no one single solution to the housing issue. Different governments have their different experiences with the implementation of their public policies. While it is accepted fact that the affordable-housing crisis impacts on communities across different markets, such local problems are not likely to go away so fast. Collaboration of government and business has been put in place, but the solution must go beyond affordability.

Community living

A more sustainable community is necessary, as demonstrated in the case of Singapore. Inclusiveness and sustainability of community building would be necessary to get the design of affordable housing right. This includes ready access to reliable public transport, and education facilities. The community must have a balanced mix of places where people can work and interact, as well as shops of all amenities and conveniences. The infrastructures must be maintained to an extent where people can carry on their way of life. Ultimately, affordable housing is not just cost alone; central to this is whether a community can be sustainable and engaging.

CHAPTER 17

The world is running out of fish

A recent AFP global news agency report on the diminishing fish stock is worrying. The fact that 90 per cent of all possible marine fish stocks are reported to be depleting at an alarming rate is already testing the limits of sustainability. The International Union for the Conservation of Nature (IUCN) singled out a number of sea and freshwater fish that are now in danger of going extinct. The UN's FAO (FAO) indicated in their June 2018 report that 30 per cent of all fish stocks are now overexploited, posing a real threat to not just the industry but also the community and society.

Reduction

Another factor contributing to reduction in fish stocks is the effects of pollution, namely constant and regular cases of oil and liquid spills, as well as poisonous chemicals being discharged into the ocean by trawlers and industries. These unethical practices have harmed the marine habitat. *National*

Geographic, in their 2006 reports, warned the global leaders and community that based on their study and data, the future is grim, and barring no change to the increase in the volume of fishing activities, the world's fish population will deplete and its related industry will collapse by the year 2048.

McKinsey studies in 2008 estimated the sector provides significant employment for 180 million people worldwide. A rough estimate showed the fish and fishery product export business was worth more than USD85 billion, while a World Bank report reminds the world that the business supplies a significant portion of animal protein consumed, especially in the emerging countries.

It is most ironic that because of rising sophistication and efficiency of the industry, there has been a rise in the catch globally. Modern trawlers today are using fish-finding sonar, which can accurately pinpoint the location of the catch. In addition, modern fishing ships are using trawl nets, drift nets, longlines (a single fishing line with numerous hooks), and other irresponsible tactics. The consequence is overfishing. The end result is that more fish are caught than the fish population can replace through natural reproduction.

Rising demand

The rising global demand for fish products has also been blamed for fast depletion of fish stocks. The rate of depletion has led to 85 per cent of global stocks depleting; at this rate, there has been not much time for replenishment. Already, experts are predicting a gloomy outlook, projecting that by the year 2050, because of overfishing, the world will run out of seafood.

Such a gloomy outlook is worrying, as there would be a high possibility of the industry going out of business. Many small-time fishermen will suffer from loss of jobs, and the global community will find itself in a shortage of an important source of protein, i.e. fish products. The disappearance of fish stocks will also threaten food security, posing a threat to the entire fishing community that relies on such industry. Many of the bigger processing plants in fish products will either go out of business or diversify into other food business, as its consequences are unhealthy and socially unacceptable.

Any immediate reduction in fish stocks means thousands, if not millions, will be deprived of such sources of food and protein. Ironically, it was the biologists and health specialists in the mid-twentieth century that advocated for more efforts to increase the abundance of protein-rich foods, which led to an abrupt increase in fishing. Consumers soon got used to having access to a variety of fish species at affordable prices— however, that affordability for consumers comes at a large cost to the oceans. Many health experts are already sounding the warning bells over the potential risk and the dangers these will pose to the communities, including the impacts of social issues and problems.

UN Sustainable Development Goals

As one of the UN Sustainable Development Goals, to conserve and use the oceans' resources sustainably is essential and necessary. Rightly so, the development goal recognises the need to protect, preserve, and sustain the consumption of marine resources in the world's oceans. Recognising the challenges, UN development goals have demanded the effective management and resources and regulations be put in place to reduce overfishing and ocean pollution and improve the quality of the water.

Marine habitat is important, as ecosystems, once disrupted, will trigger a chain reaction that would upset the balance. Imagine the ocean without planktons, for example. These are a source of food for others, and any depletion will affect the growth of others, hence the effect on overall biodiversity. What can be more damaging than to remove very source that creates the system? The vulnerable marine life hinges on survival of species that cannot be removed.

Actions

There have been numerous international multilateral talks, discussions over solutions to tackle the prevailing issues of overfishing and risk of fish disappearing from dinner plates. While governments all over the world have discussed or even drawn up maritime laws to manage fishing rights, problems of overfishing persist. It is recognised if there are effective and concerted efforts to reduce fishing activities, fish populations of all types will be allowed to replenish, and fish population can return to its peak. Quota, or putting a cap on fishing catch, is always a controversial matter, even within a collective agreement among countries, as many will find it harder to enforce than to agree on. But many governments will not disagree that multilateral agreements are necessary to ensure enforcement is effective.

In the development of aquaculture, fish farms are being created and implemented extensively as an alternative to catching them wild. According to a FAO report released in June 2018, entitled *Impacts of climate change on fisheries and aquaculture*, between 1950 and 2015, global aquaculture production grew at a mean annual rate of 7.7 per cent and, by 2016, had reached 80.0 million tonnes of food fish and 30.1 million tonnes of aquatic plants, equivalent to 53 per cent of global production of fish for food by capture fisheries and aquaculture combined.

Climate change

The effects of climate change can have direct and indirect impacts on aquaculture, both short and long term. Changing weather patterns are expected to hit production, resulting in losses and weakened infrastructure damaged by floods. FAO also predicted changing temperature increases risk of diseases, parasites, and harmful algae blooms, and harms farming conditions.

Climate change will affect precipitation in many regions, and the fast melting of snow and ice will alter the water resources in terms of quantity and quality. Rainfall patterns are projected to change everywhere, and this is expected to affect the temperature of the oceans. Ultimately, experts are predicting all of these changes to climatic conditions will alter breeding of fish, and its ecosystem.

Business response

One of the immediate responses to responsible fishing came from the World Wildlife Fund (WWF) and the Dutch Sustainable Initiative in 2010, when they helped to establish the Aquaculture Stewardship Council (ASC), an independent certifying body with global influence, in its efforts to promote responsible fishing in order to sustain the ocean's marine life. The ASC, racing against time, organises ambitious programmes to educate and transform the world's seafood markets through promotion of best environmental and social aquaculture practices. This includes the need to introduce labelling of certified responsibly produced seafood to inform buyers of the sustainability urgency, by increasing the promotion and use of the ASC logo. ASC is not alone in this journey. There is also the Marine Stewardship Council (MSC), a similar non-profit organisation formed to raise awareness of unsustainable fishing practices and to sustain seafood supply for the future.

John West, a leading player in the industry, is already committed to sustainably sourced tuna in its package and delivery of canned seafood. John West Australia, which has more than 40 per cent of the market share in Australia, has made its products to be certified by MSC as sustainably sourced, a must in its business. The decision to embrace the sustainably sourced tuna has a profound impact and influence over the whole of the canned tuna industry in Australia. It also sets a new industry benchmark and a move towards a more sustainable future for the industry.

The sustainability certification is not free from criticism. MSC was criticised for not upholding standards to reduce overfishing, in a report produced by Channel News Asia on 15 September 2018. The report alleged an increasing number of cases where controversial fisheries were certified despite evidence of unsustainable practices and environmental concerns. The news channel, in its documentary, questioned a number of so-called green practices.

Clear danger ahead

There is strong evidence that fish production is already exceeding its sustainable limit despite steps taken at regional levels. According to the UN FAO, more than 90 per cent of the fish stocks are overfished. The UN agency even singled out that a popular species like tuna is already in danger of being overfished, in its 'State of the World's Fisheries' report. While the alternative means of fish farming, aquaculture, has overtaken fish caught from the wild, there are limits and risks confronting such a method.

Aquaculture has delivered much benefit in terms of making up the supply to meet the growing consumption; it faces the challenges of climate change and possible pollution. There are also limits. For example, the breeding of shrimp has led to disappearance of natural wetlands, an important feature of the ecosystem. Twelve per cent of the world's population is involved in this industry. Majority of these are small communities concentrated in the developing nations, which will face the brunt of the climate change consequences. The immediate answer is to slow down demand, allowing the fish population to multiply, but not many are listening. It is danger ahead, especially so when majority of those affected will come from the low-income categories.

The world will soon run out of fish to satisfy growing human consumption. There is no immediate answer; only time will tell whether such sustainable development goals can be met.

CHAPTER 18

Diminishing forests

Once upon a time, at least 50 per cent of the landmass on this planet was covered with forests. Fast forward, this percentage was reduced to just under 30 per cent. Even more scary is that the World Wildlife Fund (WWF) is now predicting that the forest cover is being reduced by 1 per cent annually. According to the 2015 Global Forest Resources Assessment, the forest cover has been reduced by 50 per cent over the past three decades. Much of these losses are in the tropics.

Forest disappearance

At the 2015 Forestry Congress in Durban, South Africa, a team of scientists updated the global community that the total forest area declined by 3 per cent between 1990 and 2015, from 4,128 million hectares to 3,999 million hectares. The good news is that the annual rate of net forest loss halved from 7.3 million ha per year in the 1990s to 3.3 million ha per year between 2010 and 2015. There was a significant difference in net forest loss between climatic domains, with most deforestation occurring in the tropics. From 2010 to 2015, tropical forest area declined by 5.5 million ha per year while temperate forest area expanded at a rate of 2.2 million ha per year. The conference also shared the rapid disappearance of forests in regions of Central and South America, South and South-East Asia, and all three regions in Africa.

The diminishing forests can be blamed on logging activities, and equally devastating are conversions of the land to agricultural activities and forest fires. Official statistics show more than 70,000 forest forests were recorded in Brazil alone in the first eight months of 2019. The Brazilian Institute of Space Research confirms that the Amazon loses more than 800 square miles in one month, equivalent to two football pitches every minute.

Concerns

No one can deny the importance of the forests. They are a rich habitat for thousands of animals and plants. The land under forests is an important indicator for the FAO of the United Nations. Scientists have repeatedly reminded global leaders of the importance of forest cover, a necessary part of the ecosystem, and one that must be preserved in the ongoing global battle against climate change. The FAO have officially recognised that '*forests are important carbon pools which continuously exchange carbon dioxide with the atmosphere, due to both natural processes and human action. Understanding forests' participation in the greenhouse effect requires a better understanding of the carbon cycle at the forest level.*'

The problem of deforestation has been a global concern, but the diminishing Amazon rainforest is one of even deeper concern to United Nations. The global community's concern is well justified. The Amazon rainforest represents 30 per cent of the world's remaining green lungs. It accounts for 20 per cent of the earth's green air, and the 400 billion trees absorb carbon dioxide from earth's atmosphere.

The *Guardian* newspaper reported even as early as 11 February 2011 the destruction of rainforests and acknowledged the setback to the battle against climate change. The newspaper quoted important observations from scientists that forest loss and land activities account for around 23 per cent of current man-made CO_2 emissions—which equates to 17 per cent of the 100-year warming impact of all current greenhouse-gas emissions. It is estimated that more than 1.5 billion tons of carbon dioxide are released to the atmosphere from deforestation, mainly the cutting and burning of forests, every year.

Even the US-owned weather centre reported that over thirty million acres of forests and woodlands are lost every year due to deforestation, causing a massive loss of income to poor people living in remote areas who depend on the forest to survive.

Causes

Scientists have confirmed the research finding that dense tropical forests are best kept preserved, as they absorb large amounts of carbon pollution from atmosphere, storing them in leaves, soil, roots, etc.

Today more than 10 per cent of the global carbon dioxide emissions that contributed to problems of climate change are caused by deforestation. Forest clearing for agricultural activities is a major cause of deforestation. One contentious headline is that of palm oil cultivation.

Palm oil is singled out as a major contributor to deforestation and climate change. It is very debatable whether palm oil should solely be blamed, as the fruit itself is recognised as a source of food to millions in both developed and developing markets. It is used as an affordable ingredient to make thousands of household products from cooking oil to shampoo, and even used for baking bread and cakes. Palm oil is commonly used in fast-food chain stores and as an ingredient to make biodiesel.

A report from the US-based Union of Concerned Scientists showed livestock rearing and production took more land, as well as conversion of forestland to soya bean cultivation. Critics of palm oil also pointed that clearing and burning forest for palm oil releases large volumes of carbon monoxide. Such practices contribute to the problem of greenhouse gas emissions, blamed for a quarter of global carbon dioxide emission.

Consequences

Rainforest and peatland ecosystems conveniently store billions of tons of carbon and methane gases. The clearing of rainforest, especially in peat areas, which cover much of mainland Borneo, has been blamed as one of the causes of global warming. The Borneo forest has been recognised as one of the three lungs of the earth, yet it has not made much difference to the attitude of the governments and businesses towards agribusiness. Indeed, public protests and consultations have not made much difference.

Forest fires are common and health hazards to millions of people. Several known forest fires are due to clearing of land to make way for plantations. Much of the cultivation is commonly made legal through conversion of land, especially those in Borneo's jungle, which is also home to natives who lived and farmed on the ancestral land for centuries.

Illegal logging is another problem, especially in Indonesia, which has the world's third largest tropical forest. Destruction of the forest is devastating. International treaty such as ASEAN (Association of South East Asia Nations) Agreement on Transboundary Haze Pollution that were signed in 2002 and ratified in 2014, has no meaning if the agreement is not being taken seriously or enforced. Recent haze problem resulting from forest burning in Borneo has resulted in only exchange of blames at governmental levels. One of the alleged culprits behind such environmental hazard has been the plantation companies, where governments have been supporting and this has posed a dilemma for the latter to choose between profitable export earnings or to protect social agenda of public health and interest.

Understandably, the rate of conversion of forestland into land for agricultural activities and often housing too will not be slowing down. Ironically, the use of more sophisticated technology has enabled government and industry to quicken the forest clearing. Making choices is not difficult as national governments often do not see the immediate tangible benefits of saving the forests. Such bad publicity has attracted much criticism from many non-governmental organisations. The recent public demonstration by London's Extinction Rebellion, which paralysed the capital over one Easter week, was one of the highlights that has given palm oil growers bad publicity.

Mitigating actions

The problem of deforestation is that it harms the earth's fragile ecosystem and biodiversity, including its habitats and rare species, as well as bringing air pollution, and it could even adversely affect weather patterns. There have been mitigating actions taken by governments, including a recent proposed ban on palm oil for production of biodiesel by the European Union. As many governments already embraced and agreed to work towards a reduction of carbon emission at the climate change meeting in Paris and the agreement of a new set of sustainable development goals, the value of forests in addressing climate change and other global and national development objectives is becoming more apparent.

One of the decisions made at the 2015 Paris Climate Accord was the recognition given to a proposed forest scheme where countries' contributions to offset carbon emissions can include protecting forests or even planting trees. The European Union and several states in the US have indicated their plans to include forest planting. Others have followed suit, including Colombia, Canada, and even China, have officially announced their programme of replanting trees.

Intelligence

Despite these bold commitments, each year the world's tropical forests continue to disappear by roughly thirty-nine million acres of trees, according to a report by Global Forest Watch. To support this, forest intelligence would need to be updated and complete. While there have been improvements arising from the UN Climate Change Convention, much needs to be done. The UN Intergovernmental Panel on Climate Change, in its report before the Paris Climate Accord in 2015, confirmed the speed with which global warming has gathered pace. But a *Guardian* newspaper report of 4 October 2018 carried the headline 'Scientists say halting deforestation "just as urgent" as reducing emissions'. The report further elaborated a statement made by a group of scientists that reiterated the importance of forests in combating climate change risks had been overlooked by the world's governments. The report further echoed the fears among many that the forest fire would release three trillion tons of carbon dioxide, and by protecting and restoring forests, the earth would be able to achieve 18 per cent of the emissions mitigation targets by 2030.

The importance of forests is never in doubt. Diminishing forests will have long-term impacts, as scientists have confirmed that there is clear evidence that such destruction has contributed to an increase in global carbon emissions. The degradation of the ecosystems, largely due to man-made developments, is to be blamed.

Man-made

The importance of forests in the past has not been taken seriously, especially in countries where forests are cleared to make way for more tangible but profitable agriculture-based activities. Although palm oil has been unfairly singled out as one prime example, others including dairy farming and soya bean cultivation are equally to be blamed. One answer is to encourage sustainable agriculture, which to a large extent would halt damage to environment. This is another proposition and challenge facing both sustainability proponents and business.

CHAPTER 19

Can we live without coal?

For generations, coal has been the fuel that powered and kept the economy and society moving. However, a number of advanced nations have shifted away from such source of fuel, as coal has caused huge carbon emissions blamed for the rise in global temperature. The preference for cleaner energy is also being supported by greater accessibility to its technology and availability of cheaper gas.

Despite such trends, the overall global demand for coal consumption continues to enjoy growth. According to a report in the *Economist* newspaper of 24 August 2019, China now accounts for half the global consumption, representing more than 1,893 million tons of oil equivalent based on 2017 figures. The International Energy Agency (IEA) reports that Asia now accounts for 75 per cent of the world's consumption of the filthiest fuel. While China is both the world's producer and consumer, within the region, Japan, South Korea, and increasingly Vietnam top the chart on consumption.

Demand

Coal demand is not expected to slow in the countries of Asia, in contrast to the dip in the demand among the European countries.

On an aggregate, the European demand for coal has now dropped to fourth place behind China, India, and the United States. The decline in coal consumption in Europe is largely due to the deliberate government policy of phasing out of coal-fired power plants. In its place are the use of gas and, to an extent, renewable energy. Improvement in efficiency of fuel consumption is another reason. A more plausible explanation is that is because of government policy to substitute coal with cleaner energy as it is generally accepted that burning of coal is bad for the environment.

A much different scenario is observed in Asia. The rise in the number of coal-fired plants across China, India, and South-East Asian countries shows the government priority remains using coal as a cheap source of power. It is no surprising that a large percentage of these coal-fired plants are owned by the governments. All these countries are predicting that demand for electricity will double or even triple within the next ten years. The governments in these emerging markets see the demand trend as inevitable in order to cope with growing population demand. More coal-fired plants are expected to be built with Chinese financing in Pakistan and Bangladesh, both of whom are involved in the China Belt and Road Initiative.

The *Economist* newspaper, in its 2 August 2018 issue, reported that India is already the world's second biggest burner of coal after China. The country consumed an additional twenty-seven million tonnes, a rise of 4.8 per cent. The newspaper also reported an increase in aggregate demand for coal in China. Elsewhere, there have been big increases from Bangladesh and Pakistan to the Philippines and South Korea. Such is the supply and demand that prices for thermal coal, the type used for generating electricity, are at their highest since 2012 and have more than doubled since then.

Such a demand trend is not only confined to emerging countries in Asia. Even in the United States, coal remains the most popular fossil fuel in at least eighteen states, according to government's official statistics. The trend confirms how dependent government and business are on coal for power, jobs, and convenience.

Coal debate

Coal is the dirtiest of all available fuel. But it is cheap, and technology to extract is widely available.

The argument against the use of coal is that reducing the consumption of coal will reduce the amount of carbon emission. Targeting coal-fired plants is obvious.

One could also argue that governments in Asia are also signatories to the Paris Agreement, where they have agreed that coal-fired plants will eventually be phased out by 2030. There is no denial among the signatories that coal, as one of the fossil fuels, is bad for global warming.

The same argument is used in Australia, where the power plants are expected to be replaced by clean energy by 2050. Up to 80 per cent of electricity demand is expected to be met by renewable energy largely solar, biomass, and even wind. The Australian planners are expected to push for new technology in solar energy to be used; at the same time, coal-fired power plants will be gradually phased out.

These developments are in response to repeated warnings from scientists that the world needs to stop fossil-fuel use, including coal, by 2100 if climate change is to be avoided. It is in line with one of the United Nations Sustainable Development Goals, which seeks to ensure access to affordable, reliable, sustainable, and modern energy for all by 2030.

The argument put forth by governments in these emerging countries is that almost 1.2 billion people have access to electricity since the year 2000, and the number of people without access to electricity fell to about 1.0 billion in 2016. According to the IEA, these developments took place in two countries, where 500 million were beneficiaries in India and 900 million people in China.

The alternative form of energy is to have more wind and solar installations to generate cleaner energy, but arguments against these are both financial and non-financial. First, it has always been argued that the steep cost of investment is a deterrent, but moreover, it is less reliable, as none of the countries in Asia can have reliable access to sunshine or wind. However, cheaper cost of renewable energy technology plus a deliberate push by financial institutions committed to fund clean energy that offers brighter hopes for the future.

Finally, it is the government commitment that is the key to the future of the coal industry. The *Economist* newspaper, in its commentary, has said that fate of the climate will be sealed if governments in both China and India continue to invest in coal-fired power plants and ignore the perils of the climate change.

It is fair to say that any possible plans to replace coal would not happen so soon.

Campaign

The dependence on coal as well as gas and oil are well founded, and switching to a more sustainable energy, for example, solar, water, or even wind has so far been confined to a handful of countries; some may already have achieved their 100 per cent renewable energy goal. This is also partly the result of campaign against dirty energy such as coal.

To a large extent, the environmental pressure groups have achieved a considerable success including policymakers at multiple levels. Perhaps, it is argued, phasing out of coal will take place as soon as alternative sources of renewable energy are available in terms of accessibility, reliability, and price competitiveness.

Challenges

The issue is also on funding. Renewable energy, for example, that requires both technology and natural source but an investment to the tune of almost USD1 trillion is not surprising.

The International Energy Agency's view that the world should restrain from burning their oil, gas, and coal is also not practical. Such a view appears impractical and unrealistic. The challenge is whether the effort to put coal off limits will be bound to fail. It is therefore not incorrect to suggest that coal resources will remain an essential part of the energy mix in the near future.

It is one thing to recognise that it is impossible to even suggest that reducing coal in a country's energy will take place any time in the next twenty years. It is another thing to consider the ramifications of turning a blind eye to a cheap source of energy such as coal.

Although coal is polluting and dirty, many countries, including India, are highly dependent on it. Today, it provides almost 8 per cent of the country's electricity. The industry also employs more than 500,000 workers across its production supply chain. Coal is also being used to power the national rails, which not only provide convenience to millions of travellers across India, but also are one of the country's largest employers.

A similar story appears in Indonesia, the fifth largest carbon emitter. The country is still reliant on coal for its power plants despite attempts to increase its renewable energy. Another reason for the slowdown in the latter is the costly investment to switch to renewable energy, and besides, the supply of renewable energy is perceived as unreliable and impractical.

It is obvious European countries have taken the lead to transit from the use of coal for power generation to renewable energy. The shift towards clean energy is obvious; many have already enjoyed the benefits. Austria, Norway, Iceland are moving towards 100 per cent renewable by 2050.

The shift includes too the creation of new jobs in the renewable energy sector. Even the financial services industry is reported to be helping the financing towards the installation of renewable energy technology and, at the same time, limiting the same benefits to coal industry.

Future trends

Although China is one of the largest consumers of coal, the country is also the largest producer of clean energy technology, including solar panels and wind turbines.

The country is the world's investor in clean energy, especially in places where they have access to natural supplies of wind, water, or sun. Its share of renewable energy is expected to hit 16 per cent by the year 2020. The United Nations reported in 2017 that China invested almost USD126 billion on renewable sources of energy, almost half the world's expenditure of USD280 million.

Such development represents positive change. One example of such change is the city of Handan, located in the south-west province of Hebei in China. Handan today has been transformed from one of the most polluted cities, to be named as the nation's city of national garden. Handan for decades was known as a city of coal, because of its huge abundance of coal resources, and naturally, this led to development of its steel industry. Today, Handan has been revived, with millions spent on new parks, planting of trees, creation of more than 10,000 hectares of green parks, and clearing up of its polluted rivers and air. These are positive signs. China is committed to reducing its carbon footprint, and despite what its coal consumption statistics tend to suggest, the country has made significant steps to address the twin problems of pollution and carbon emissions.

Elsewhere in Asia, the consumption of coal appears to be holding up despite the commitment of various governments to switch to cleaner energy. The relentless campaigns against coal may have succeeded in the advanced markets outside United States.

The staying power is obvious. Its substitute, renewable energy, is regarded to be costly and often unreliable. The access to natural supplies is one thing, but consumer choice is largely determined by price sensitivity. The good thing is that prices may be coming down for both solar panel and wind installations. Aside from the economies, it is also about the practicality. These installations require physical infrastructures. The production of solar energy depends on the reliability and availability of sunshine; not all geographies have such physical advantages.

Governments, especially those in parliamentary democracies, want to keep their promises to their constituencies. Coal-fired plants are generally regarded to be more reliable to allow the convenience of electricity. Consumers may not be too bothered with the fuel used to generate the electricity.

Until the environment becomes unbearable, majority will not be too concerned. It is also expected that public will start making their feelings known when effects of climate change start affecting their livelihoods. Until these are overcome, the case for the use of coal continues.

Overall, it does look as if the region has got out of its dependence on coal. It looks like many cannot live without coal at least for a while, and this remains a worry for many sustainability supporters.

Experts do expect the market share for coal will decline. But many believe change will not happen so soon. For the coming decade, it looks like in most parts of Asia, governments will place business and social priorities ahead of environment.

Governments may have agreed and committed to a 2-degrees Celsius target ceiling, but there remains the issue on national agenda, which has been given more priority.

CHAPTER 20

Plastic addiction

Aquaman, the blockbuster movie from Warner Brothers, carries a strong environmental message that reminds the global community that the oceans are suffering from rampant pollution damage resulting from the carelessness and decadence of human lifestyle. Much of the pollution comes from plastic waste that people and society have been producing from the convenience and comfort of modern lifestyle and activities. Plastic is the main culprit, cheap to produce and versatile to use, but the seven-billion-plus inhabitants on earth have become so addicted, especially to one-time use, that these have resulted in severe environmental consequences.

Plenty of plastic waste

According to *National Geographic*, the challenge of plastic addiction is so well documented that each year, an estimated eighteen billion pounds of plastic waste enters the world's ocean from coastal regions. Even more astonishing, *National Geographic* estimates that an equivalent of five grocery bags of plastic trash ends up on every foot of coastline on the planet. Tons of plastic debris will cause much harm to the fragile ecosystem in the ocean, from coral reefs to even large whales and even seagulls that often mistake these plastic bits for food.

There are now fresh findings from research that shows plastic pollution is also harming both social and economic sustainability, including a threat to humanity's food security.

It is estimated that one million plastic drinking bottles are bought every single minute—that it is no exaggeration up to five trillion plastic bags are used in one single year. Another 40 per cent of all plastic produced, according to *National Geographic*, is used in packaging, and much of that is used only once and then discarded.

The Earth Day Network, a non-profit organisation that operates in more than a hundred countries, stepped up their campaign against environment degradation and their strong advocacy for green conservation and climate activism. One of their recent campaigns is not only to raise awareness through education but also to engage local leaders and organisations to champion for an end to plastic pollution and campaign for cleaner energy. It produces a fact sheet that tells how plastic is proving dangerous to our planet, health, and wildlife. The fact sheet as part of their education campaign reinforces the main survey findings and observations that have attracted attention from many governments.

| Fact # 1 | About 8 million metric tons of plastic are thrown into the ocean annually. Of those, 236 thousand tons are microplastics—tiny pieces of broken-down plastic smaller than your little fingernail. |

Fact # 2	There are five massive patches of plastic in the oceans around the world. These huge concentrations of plastic debris cover large swaths of the ocean; the one between California and Hawaii is the size of the state of Texas.
Fact # 3	Every minute, one garbage truck of plastic is dumped into our oceans.
Fact # 4	The amount of plastic in the ocean is set to increase tenfold by 2020.
Fact # 5	By 2050, there will be more plastic in the oceans than there are fish.
Fact # 6	Plastic is found in the ocean as far as 11 km deep, meaning synthetic fibres have contaminated even the most remote places on Earth.
Fact # 7	Many marine organisms can't distinguish common plastic items from food. Animals that eat plastic often starve because they can't digest the plastic which fills their stomachs, preventing them from eating real food.
Fact # 8	The likelihood of coral becoming diseased increases from 4 per cent to 89 per cent after encountering marine plastic. It also damages the skin of coral, allowing infection. Coral reefs are home to more than 25 per cent of marine life.

Fact # 9	There is more plastic than natural prey at the sea surface of the Great Pacific Garbage Patch, which means that organisms feeding at this area are likely to have plastic as a major component of their diets. For instance, sea turtles by-caught in fisheries operating within and around the patch can have up to 74 per cent (by dry weight) of their diets composed of ocean plastics.
Fact # 10	Many fish humans consume, including brown trout, cisco, and perch, have at one time or another, ingested plastic microfibres. Source: Earth Day Network Fact Sheet: Plastics in the Ocean

Another non-profit organisation, Plastic Oceans International, whose mission is to educate the public of the dangers of plastic pollution and to influence and change global attitude and consumer behaviours, is convinced plastic pollution is an unnecessary and unsustainable waste of resource. Its summary of research findings once again reaffirms the fact that consumer behaviour and lifestyle have adverse consequences.

1. Packaging is the largest end-use market segment, accounting for just over 40 per cent of total plastic usage.

2. Annually, approximately 500 billion plastic bags are used worldwide. More than 1 million bags are used every minute.

3. A plastic bag has an average working life of fifteen minutes.

4. Over the last ten years, we have produced more plastic than during the whole of the last century.

    Beverage Bottles Alone

5. According to the Container Recycling Institute, 100.7 billion plastic beverage bottles were sold in the US in 2014, or 315 bottles per person.

6. Fifty-seven per cent of those units were plastic water bottles: 57.3 billion sold in 2014. This is up from 3.8 billion plastic water bottles sold in 1996, the earliest year for available data.

7. The process of producing bottled water requires around six times as much water per bottle as there is in the container.

8. Fourteen per cent of all litter comes from beverage containers. When caps and labels are considered, the number is higher.

Source: Plastic Oceans website

Alarm bells

The United Nations, in their recent survey, shows that only 9 per cent of all plastic waste ever produced is being recycled, while much of the waste ends up in landfills.

Interestingly, the UN survey shows cigarettes butts' tiny plastic filters were found in the environment, while the most common ones are bottle caps, wrappers, straws, drink lids, and even stirrers. Many consumers have no idea where these ended up!

The addiction to plastic material is an understatement, as it is hard to imagine a day without the use of plastic. The material is part of the mainstream and seemingly irreplaceable to industry and society. Imagine housewives without plastic to wrap and store their food materials. This is hardly surprising as the *Daily Telegraph* newspaper on 19 July 2019 reported that oversized plastic packaging was being used to wrap food contents half its size. It is also common to find traders using them for takeaways. Even industry will find it difficult to function without plastic material. Perhaps more and more users and producers are using more recyclable materials.

The rate of plastic production has been growing phenomenally. Plastic has been the preferred material over the past five decades because it is economical and durable, and even more worrying, all of these were meant to be thrown away after one use.

Experts predicted that if the current consumption is left uncontrolled, the plastic industry by 2050 will consume one fifth of world's total oil consumption. By the same token, experts are also predicting that the oceans could end up having more plastic than fish population.

Government

Managing plastic waste is now taken seriously by many developed nations; many have substantially reduced the production and use, especially single use. While the governments in the more advanced markets have acted, the

United Nations survey reports show the emerging markets of China and South-East Asia account for half of the plastic waste that ended up in the oceans. Already many governments have banned outright plastic carrier bags that are meant for single use. Some African states have banned outright use of plastic bags, while in Malaysia, there is already a ban on the use of plastic straws. China, both a large producer and consumer of plastic, prohibited the import of plastic waste for recycling.

Corporations such as Coca-Cola, Unilever, Procter & Gamble, and McDonald's were all reported to have pledged to use more recycled materials, but how much of these would translate into tangible benefits is anyone's guess. The increase in economic activities has resulted in increased tons, and according to a recent *Economist* report, of the current 6.3 billion tonnes of plastic waste, only 9 per cent has been recycled and another 12 per cent incinerated. The rest ends up in landfills. Much of these are small items, from plastic cups to wrappers, that ended up being exported until recently to China.

Malaysia was one of the countries that were swamped by plastic waste that got nowhere. Demand for such plastic waste was based on one of the beliefs that these plastic wastes could present a business opportunity for those in the recycling business. But not all these plastic uses could be recycled, and many of the plants, often illegal, were found to be burning the waste, hence harming the environment more. This has led to the Malaysian government imposing an immediate ban on such imports.

The *Guardian* newspaper, on 29 March 2019, reported a significant decision by the European Union towards legislating on the reduction of use of food containers and plastic lids for hot drinks. By 2025, it is expected plastic bottles will be made with at least 25 per cent recycled content, and by 2029, recycled material will be used for such convenience. The European parliament also agreed to outright ban on single-use plastic cutlery, even cotton buds and drinking straws, all of which have been accused as culprits for ocean pollution. Frans Timmermans, a European Commission vice president who led the initiative, was quoted to have said, 'Today we have taken an important step to reduce littering and plastic pollution in our oceans and seas. We got this; we can do this. Europe is setting new and ambitious standards, paving the way for the rest of the world.'

Consequences

Poor plastic waste collection has led to huge discharge of the dangerous materials into main rivers all around the world. These rivers provide sources of water to communities whose livelihood depends on access to water in the rivers. The *Economist* reported that in October 2018, the Helmholtz Centre for Environmental Research in Germany found that ten main rivers, including two in Africa and the rest in Asia, discharge 90 per cent of all plastic marine debris, making them major culprits to ocean pollution. The United Nations found that each year, a staggering eight million tonnes of plastic flow through the rivers and end up in the oceans.

It is now common knowledge plastic waste has affected marine life, and some of these include sea turtles; even large whales have been reported to have been killed by plastics which ended up in their stomachs. All of these have raised alarm bells of the adverse impact to the food chain, and eventually a threat to humanity.

There is no doubt that plastic waste becomes a problem when these remain uncollected or disposed haphazardly. The traditional landfill methods have their own limitations, and many governments have now started to act through their respective legislations to ban outright the use of plastic.

Meanwhile, the consumption of plastic continues to remain high; indeed, in many cases, the demand is almost inelastic. While recycling policy and ban on certain plastic products will help, they will not significantly change the amount of plastic waste that goes into the ocean.

A massive clean-up of the oceans has started, where solid plastic waste is being picked up from oceans and transported to land for recycling purposes. Until science and technology make plastic waste removal and management easier, a combination of policies and education would be necessary, ensuring greater sustainability of Earth's precious resources in oceans.

CHAPTER 21

Missing climate targets

At the Paris climate convention, 12 December 2015, a total of 174 governments and the European Union collectively agreed to combat climate change through a broad range of actions including investment towards a low-carbon future. Such a historic milestone is significant as it brings together all nations, big and small, with a common goal to overcome the dangers of climate change.

The agreement gives the global community a broad framework to work on limiting global temperature rise to no more than 2°C, and to get there, the convention agreed to a set of objectives and proposed mitigating actions and adaptation policies towards the development of low-carbon economies.

The Paris Agreement is historic but very relevant since the first Earth Summit in Rio de Janeiro 1992, when the United Nations Conference on Environment and Development made its first declaration to protect the integrity of the global environment and the development system.

Two decades forward, the Paris Agreement gives the world a fresh start towards addressing the perils of climate change. All participating countries have agreed to move in the same direction towards common goals and targets, to tackle the adverse impacts of climate change, and to provide better access towards financing the appropriate investments in low-carbon technologies to ensure a much climate-resilient pathway.

Achieving these goals will demand appropriate mobilisation and provision of human and financial resources, robust technology, and system framework to be put in place across many developing countries and countries most prone to effects of climate change.

2018

All nations went home to undertake respective tasks as agreed at Paris. Three years on, at its conference of parties (Cop24) climate change gathering in Katowice in Poland, 2018, more than 22,000 delegates from all member countries converged to take stock of the bold initiatives agreed in Paris. To the disappointment of media and observers, the UNFCCC (United Nations Framework Convention on Climate Change) informed the conference that not a single country was on track to meet the country's voluntary target to hold the temperature rise of no more than 2°C. Instead, fresh data on climate indicators showed the world is on track to break its promise of limiting the amount of greenhouse gas emission. The average rise in temperature is now expected to hit as high as 3°C over the next twelve years.

Such a bearish prediction came at a time when several of the big greenhouse emitters were already in place to go green across their economic and social policies. The *New York Times* reported in its 7 December 2018 issue: 'It is plain we are way off course,' said António Guterres, the secretary general of the United Nations, in a speech in Katowice this week. 'We are still not doing enough, nor moving fast enough, to prevent irreversible and catastrophic climate disruption.'

Not meeting the targets has always been a challenge. One reason is that the Paris deal is voluntary and not legally binding. Self-imposed targets, while empowering, are meant to give a better chance of success. The voluntary agreement among nations by itself is dependent on several external factors, chief among them political will and investment. The Climate Action Tracker data analysis shared its pessimistic forecasts by insisting that if every individual country fulfilled its pledges the earth is still on track to become hotter, way in excess of the limit of two degrees.

A brief description follows on the progress of selected nations with high CO_2 emissions and the rest of the world towards their efforts on their promises at the climate conferences.

United States

The United States was one of the major economies to commit to the Paris Climate Accord, but Donald Trump upon becoming its forty-fifth president on 20 January 2017 reversed its decision. The US is one of the world's largest economies and major producer of greenhouse gas. But the new President Donald Trump is not convinced of the climate change threats.

Instead, the new US President was adamant of his policies to revive the steel and auto industries as well as coal industry and fuel-powered vehicles. All of these did not augur well for the country's stand and commitment to go green.

The country is already well below the minimum expectation of an advanced nation, and it would not be easy for US to catch up with rest of its contemporaries. Based on a CNN report, 8 January 2019, carbon emissions increased in the United States by 3.4 per cent in 2018 after a few years of decline. This was disclosed in an independent economic policy research report, which also indicated the main source came from power and transport sectors.

China

In contrast, China made a pledge at Paris that it has no intention to break, and most observers believe China's demand for fossil fuels, including coal, will peak in the year 2030. China today is saddled with environmental concerns, as they have been a big consumer of fossil fuels largely blamed for the problem of greenhouse gas.

The country, however, wants to reverse this negative impression. China is the biggest market for electric-powered cars, and it has the world's best network of electric-run rail and more electric buses than anywhere in the world. China's investment in renewable energy has been increasing over the years. Take for example its renewable power capacity, which rose, according to Reuters, by 12 per cent in 2018, reflecting the deliberate strategy to reduce its dependence on coal, and its commitment to reduce greenhouse gas emissions. There are still plans for China to maximise its capacity using solar technology as well as hydroelectric.

United Kingdom

The United Kingdom has been a strong proponent towards a low-carbon economy, but the government has not able to achieve its own targets. Despite the noticeable reduction through the reduction of traditional carbon producers in mining, heavy industries, and power plants, there was no progress in the building and agricultural sectors of the economy. The authorities also struggled to contain the increase in carbon emission from a growing aviation industry. The Climate Change Committee, however, has made it lawful for emissions to be cut by 80 per cent by 2050, although the details have not been spelled out as there are targets that some may regard as not going far enough.

The rest of the world

The highly populated countries of India, Brazil, and Indonesia do not represent the rest of the world. But together, these countries represent the top ten users of fossil fuels and therefore a large carbon footprint that could make a difference. Both India and Brazil made many promises in Paris.

India, for example, was realistic with their promises made. It is commendable to know the country has made some progress with renewable energy, especially solar, because of the falling price of technology, and min-hydro. But India is still one of the biggest consumers of coal used to generate electricity. India still relies on cheap coal to power their power plants, and a combination of economic and social reasons are drawbacks to their ambition of reducing their carbon footprint.

Both Brazil and Indonesia are homes to huge tropical forests. They do provide not just a cover for world's carbon resource but are the best defence against climate change. Remove the cover through deforestation by either land clearing or forest fire, and the earth will see the release of carbon into the air, making it worse for climate change. In a study by the University of Maryland and World Resources Institute, the year 2017 saw the second worst year of tropical deforestation; a total of almost forty million acres perished.

Tropical trees are natural consumers of carbon dioxide, a function that aids human emissions, and experts believe the world's forests helped to suck one third of human-induced CO_2 emission. That makes it even more imperative that both Brazil and Indonesia should accept their moral duty to safeguard the tropical forests. Indonesia does have to balance between conserving their forests and the business-motivated palm oil planters. The government has also struggled to ban forest clearing as well as to phase out coal-fired power plants. Despite this, the Indonesian government's Low Carbon Development Initiative is committed to push for more efficient driven energy systems, as they are convinced that this would not reduce greenhouse gas emissions by almost 50 per cent by 2030 but it would contribute an average of 6 per cent GDP growth annually.

International agencies have offered to assist with mitigating and adaptation programmes. One of these involves use of funding or carbon credits to introduce a more sustainable forest management, involving the offer of aid to help poor farmers, and the use of standards to conserve the older forests.

Losing sleep

The case of missing climate targets is worrying, to say the least. One of those agencies losing sleep would be the IPCC, which warned global leaders that even allowing global temperature to rise 1.5°C above the pre-industrial levels would bring grave repercussions, involving frequent flooding in low-lying countries and loss of ecosystems in many parts of the world, within the next decade.

Many global leaders have accepted that adaptation strategies would need to be more practical. This includes emphasis on investment in clean energy technologies, including those that could be used to absorb carbon from the atmosphere. Good progress has been made by Iceland, Sweden, and Denmark in their efforts to reduce their carbon footprint.

The Republic of Ireland has gone one step further when their Parliament in May 2019 declared a climate and biodiversity emergency. The UK Parliament did the same about the same time, while Scotland has reset its target to zero by the year 2045. By declaring climate emergency, government legislators will be forced to enlarge and make a number of areas carbon neutral.

Many are convinced of the dangers of climate change and find it hard to ignore the adverse effects as seen in frequent and unpredictable weather in many countries.

Disclosure and transparency

Despite not meeting the Paris targets, the climate conference in Katowice, Poland saw a tougher set of carbon reduction targets being accepted. But the conference agreed a more transparent reporting would be needed to demonstrate greater consistency in measures and actions taken by each of the governments in their efforts to limit CO_2. It is left to be seen, at least from the perspectives of the climate activists, if they could now hold governments more accountable over their responsibilities, through better disclosures.

The voluntary nature of the agreement depends on political goodwill and cooperation. The global community also must move on without the United States, at least for the time being. For many conference delegates, they now have more clarity over the implementation plans, and it is also inevitable the carbon market will help many developing countries with the possible resources as well as handholding to achieve their targets and a better transit to a low-carbon economy. For now, meeting climate targets remains a challenge.

CHAPTER 22

Runaway climate change: are we prepared?

At the launch of the New Climate Economy on 12 September 2018, the UN secretary general António Guterres warned member states that the runaway climate change is a real possibility if actions taken to prevent severe repercussions do not go far enough or are simply not effective enough.

He backed up his strong words with examples of unpredictable extreme weather that are a more frequent, violent, and real threat to communities. There is a general agreement that climate change has to do with the hurricane Florence that brought much damage and misery to the communities in the state of Carolina, United States.

Extreme weather patterns saw Japan recording its hottest summer for more than seventy years in 2018. The *Times* magazine, in its 19 July 2019 issue, covered the report by the National Oceanic and Atmosphere Administration (NOAA) of the increase in the global temperature of 1.71 degrees Fahrenheit. The report of NOAA quoted a statement made by its leading climatologist that the *'climate is warming with a new global temperature record being set five times, a new normal.'* The report is consistent with other observations that summer temperature of 2019 broke its previous records in places as far as Alaska, Madagascar, New Zealand, Mexico, Western Canada, and East Asia.

Recent reports of the breaking up of ice shelf in the Antarctic, frequent flooding in the most unexpected places, and frequent outbreak of forest fires are evidences that have kept planners and environmental experts awake.

Food security

Adverse weather patterns from climate change represent a threat to any nation's food security. Disruption to the economics of food grains are to be expected each time supplies are affected by the least predictable changes to climate conditions. Any increase in the price of staple grains will certainly affect the cost of livestock feed, leading to eventual global increase in food prices and hence put more pressure on the millions of people who live and work on small farms especially in emerging countries. Not too long ago, prices of wheat grain skyrocketed because of prolonged drought in Russia and unexpected flooding in Pakistan.

Experts are naturally worried that the lack of global leadership to effectively address such sustainability concern will bring about even worse consequences for the global communities. But the worry is also over the worsening environmental conditions, for example, intensity of climate change that makes any adaptation plans redundant; hence, runaway climate change is inevitable.

Tipping point

Many low-lying countries will not be spared from the intense impact of climate change. Recent flooding and landslide disasters in India and Bangladesh demonstrated the extent of damage what unusual weather could do to communities. No scientist can accurately predict the consequences of climate change, but science is seldom proven wrong. Many believe the earth will experience more intense severity of extreme climate change events. In other words, floods taking place in unexpected places are just a tipping point and pose a risk to both business and social communities.

There are fears among concerned bodies and individuals, including non-governmental organisations, that the climate change agenda will not get the priority it deserves, as many governments including local legislators continue to push for business priorities, especially cost factor, ahead of any proposed changes. Any attempt to replace the easy access of fossil fuel or even replace cheaply produced plastic will not be easy. It is obvious that the shift away from the high-carbon lifestyle that is convenient and cheaper will not be easy.

Government can do more

Most emerging countries prefer the advanced markets to take the lead in the global battle against climate change. Many justified their reason by simply using their low per capita income as well as their share of carbon emissions. But many simply may not have access to the right low-carbon technology and investments.

Governments, however, must set the tone if they want to lead in this battle against global problem. Commitments made at Paris climate protocol are not legally binding. Indeed, recent change in government policies towards preservation of forests in Amazon basin shows how unpredictable government can be. The non-governmental organisations have openly said many of the commitments towards development of green-related technology haven't gone far enough. Indeed, it has been a fact that unless the commitments are legally binding, the world will have to be prepared for sudden change of position of any of the governments represented at the climate protocols.

Jobs losses

As the problem of climate change continues to worsen, the International Labour Organization (ILO) in its 2019 report *Working on a Warmer Planet: The Impact of Heat Stress on Labour Productivity*, predicted huge productivity losses involving job losses equivalent to 80 million full-time in just one decade. The ILO supports its conservative argument using the assumption that the rise in global temperature be capped at 1.5 degrees Celsius. It is also worrying, as most observers would agree that the rise in global temperature could possibly be higher, bringing greater negative impact.

Financial impacts

There are, however, groups of experts who believe that the absence of real change to climate change actions will bring about even bigger financial impacts. The Euro news in its issue of 2 July 2019 reported a headline on an important message from an international conference in Dalian, China, that immediate action is necessary to avoid a possible financial crisis from effects of climate change. An important message is that runaway climate change has become an economic opportunity for fresh investment in mitigating actions, or else a correlation between climate change and another financial crisis is a real possibility.

Legislate the change

If the governments are serious over the agenda of saving society from environmental disasters, legislating the change is necessary. A committee to oversee this is necessary; these targets include lowering the use of coal to generate electricity and a big push for electric cars and public transport as clear examples. It is not only government legislations that are necessary to support the climate change agenda, but also business and society must account for their role and responsibility towards environmental sustainability. More enforcement would be needed, and this includes making consumers change their habits towards a green lifestyle.

Unless and until nations are prepared to embrace real sustainability changes that must include environment and social changes, readiness and commitment should not be taken for granted in the war against runaway climate change.

The world will then need to be prepared for the consequences of runaway climate change. That's worrying.

CHAPTER 23

Rubbish, waste, and sustainability

According to a World Bank report 'What a Waste' released in March 2012, major global cities around the world generate 1.3 billion tonnes of municipal solid waste (MSW) per year. The volume is expected to rise to 2.2 billion tonnes by 2025.

MSW is combined household and commercial rubbish made up of everyday waste items that are thrown away by the consuming society. In the United States, these are known as trash or garbage. The United States, as the world's most affluent nation, is also the leading producer of MSW, despite having just 5 per cent of the world's population. It is widely reported that United States alone produces more than 240 million tonnes of MSW annually, and many do not expect the figures to come down. The US accumulates at least 236 million tonnes per year of MSW alone, according to the US Environmental Protection Agency.

Waste lifestyle

Observers are quick to point out the reasons for high level of wasted food in United States, one being the easy access to cheaper food than anywhere else. Second, the habits of over-buying are hard for shoppers to get rid of in United States. Indeed, the habit of discarding uneaten food is just part of the reasons.

The United Nations Food and Agriculture Organization (FAO) estimated one third of all food grown is lost or wasted, valued at nearly three trillion US dollars per year. The rising level of trash and waste worldwide is obvious, given the rising population and economic activities coming from rising consumption and production to support the increased social and economic developments. MSW are from domestic and municipal consumption of goods, manufacturing, construction, sewage treatment, and the production and disposal of hazardous substances. Waste including paper, plastics, glass, metals, foods, chemicals, oils, bricks, wood, soil, and effluent comes from all sorts of economic activities, but most waste comes from any single production by humans; these include food, oils, cooking fats, hazardous materials, vehicle oils, etc.

The rapid urbanisation that has taken place in many countries has worsened the condition. The increasing heaps of waste are potential health hazards and pollution risk to environment. The more waste that is being produced, the more landfills have to be found, or in many cases, use of energy to burn through incinerators.

Despite recycling being encouraged and now more so in a circular economy, less than 20 per cent of the waste produced are recycled. The reuse concept is also not able to keep up with the rising production of consumables. Waste disposal becomes then the most convenient way, but not everything can be got rid of through incinerators or burial in landfills, the most common ways of waste disposal.

Policies and best practices

Effective waste management is one of the to-do activities for countries to achieve the goals of the 2030 Agenda for Sustainable Development. Sustainable waste management encourages the generation of less waste, the reuse of consumables, and the recycling and recovery of waste that is produced.

The United Kingdom has a national waste strategy that is sustainable development friendly. Based on the European Union model, the practice is not only mindful of the environmental impacts of waste disposal, the process has a 3R approach: reuse, recycling, and recovery in that order of priority.

Growing pains

The level of waste generation has risen at an alarming rate, especially in advanced markets; for example, in the United States, one resident on average of more than 1,600 pounds of waste per year.

The *Economist*'s special report on waste, 29 September 2018 issue, highlights the growing pains, and challenges of coping with the growing piles of rubbish. While acknowledging the limitations of the solutions, the report is a reminder of the repercussions of growing population and affluence of nations. The newspaper regards the growing waste as a threat to public health, an environmental hazard, and an urban concern.

It is a common problem to all urban policy planners. Indian cities, for example, are among the world's largest garbage producers, generating as much as 62 million tonnes of waste each year. This figure is expected to hit 165 million tonnes, according to government sources. Indeed, it is now well known that India's tallest rubbish mountain, in the capital city of New Delhi, is predicted to rise higher than their famous Taj Mahal!

The special report pinpoints that there are three possibilities that people can do with waste: bury, burn, or recycle. But it is the economics of each of these requires a rethink of public policy. All of them bring environmental and financial implications and careful consideration. The report prefers the use of fiscal measures, using taxes for example, at production rather than recycling, as the hidden costs are often ignored. The report however agrees that since waste is socially unacceptable to the public, there is little worry over politics.

Burying waste

The practice of burying waste in landfills is common and convenient, but it brings major risks. Aside from having to find unused land, it brings unnecessary risks to human health and safety. Besides, landfills are not exactly welcomed by nearby residents because of the smell and noise, and trash brings household waste including unwanted food that produces methane when it rots. Methane is a greenhouse gas that is more potent than carbon dioxide. The changing composition of waste is not only polluting; it releases toxins that are harmful to environment and water. Household waste is not just food and papers; every household in all developed and emerging markets throws away unused paint, used batteries and light bulbs and electronic goods which contain lead and hazardous substances harmful to the environment. Industrial waste including those from mining, manufacturing, and hospitals also contain harmful toxic substances. Generally, waste is categorised into household and commercial waste; an average of 30 per cent is recyclable, and the rest of it goes to landfills.

Concerns

Waste disposal has attracted attention from the global bodies such as United Nations. The global body estimates that the world discards up to fifty million tonnes of electronic goods, or e-waste, annually.

Greenpeace is also concerned with disposal of radioactive or hazardous waste. Less than 30 per cent of these are recycled. Much of these wastes ends up in poor countries where the poor would separate and pick up discarded old mobile phones, computers, and televisions to extract valuable metals for recycling, releasing more harmful substances in the process. Greenpeace has made claims that high levels of harmful lead are found in the people who were exposed to such health hazards.

Recycling business

It is also a common practice for advanced markets to export their waste. The global waste trade, worth billions, often exports from developed countries to countries in Africa, Asia, and Latin America. Typically, the ones which export are the advanced markets; the primary purpose is often recycling or disposal. These include toxic or hazardous wastes where such burden becomes a problem.

Based on a study by a shipping consultant, 40 per cent of containers that docked at US ports returned to China with wastepaper and scrap metal. Until recently, China was one of the biggest recipients of such trash, especially from the US market. The noble purpose was for the recipient country, in this case, China, to do the recycling in a major way, and trash became a cheap source of materials for recycling. The recycling of this waste has grown big enough, despite the health risks, in the Philippines, India, and Bangladesh.

According to the *Economist* newspaper of 15 June 2019, the trash business is worth USD24 billion a year. But when China shut its door to such cheap imports, much if not all of these wastes turned up at the ports in Thailand, Malaysia, and the Philippines. More than forty illegal plastic recycling plants were spotted, and non-government organisations and even the government have expressed concern. The governments in these South-East Asian nations were not amused and ordered the return of thousands of tonnes of waste to the United Kingdom, Canada, and Australia.

The example in Malaysia exemplified the problem of waste disposal. Exports of waste have been on the rise. Reuters reported earlier that annual imports of plastic scrap into Malaysia jumped to 450,000–500,000 tonnes in 2017 from 288,000 tonnes in 2016. Countries with less strict environment law enforcement are easy targets. Malaysia, Vietnam, Indonesia, and Thailand are among the South-East Asian countries that were identified as easy targets.

A major problem from the imports is the poor standards of waste management, which includes, among others, outdated knowledge, poor or inaccurate data on waste composition, inefficient storage and collection systems, disposal of unused wastes, and inefficient utilisation of disposal site space.

Managing waste

It is time that waste management is recognised as a high priority for global sustainable development efforts. To support the growing developments and population, and since waste is being produced daily, intergovernmental actions will be necessary to recognise that waste management is a vital concern for global sustainable development.

The proliferation of plastic waste is one example. It has been proven that plastic waste not only is harmful to marine life, including large mammals such as whales, it will destroy the entire ecosystem which the earth is dependent on. Not only does waste bring negative effects to environment, improper solid waste management is not good news to climate change impact—decomposing waste produces methane in landfills and poison gas releases greenhouse gas to the air.

Effective solutions

Waste policies in many countries involve landfills and, to some extent, recycling efforts, aiming to minimise the negative effects from the generation and management of waste on human and environmental health. In many cases, this requires reduction, recovery, reuse, recycling before disposal can be considered an environmentally friendly and economically viable option. Reducing the need for landfills goes together with boosting recycling and recovery.

The UN guidelines for National Waste Management Strategies define the working framework for national governments to address their challenges. Waste management is often a local concern, but national governments will need to work with their relevant stakeholders so that their efforts are in line with the sustainable development framework.

The guidelines reiterated the importance of choices towards effective implementation of waste management. While the 3R concept of reduce, recycle, and reuse continues to underpin the approach, effective waste management discourages disposal through landfills, wherever possible.

There are no simple solutions, as the challenges are multidisciplinary. While stakeholder education and developments will help raise awareness, this is one challenge which takes long-term solutions. The concept of responsible recycling has started to gain traction in a circular economy.

There are, however, responsible companies that made positive and transparent steps on recycling their production wastes. Hewlett-Packard, Canon, Agilent Technologies are a few examples of these companies that made efforts to collect and recycle their wastes, some of which are hazardous to the public.

Important innovations are substituting many harmful plastics, for example. The use of biodegradable materials for wrapping food, changing lifestyle towards food consumption, and the use of fiscal measures in managing waste are all part of integrated strategy.

There are some signs of newer and bolder inventions that use organic material for food packaging, and if this succeeds, it will solve half the world's problem of plastic waste. Only time will tell.

CHAPTER 24

Circular economy—opportunity or fad?

There has been a lot of concerns over the excessive consumption in most major economies. Consumption has been regarded as a necessary demand factor towards growth and prosperity. But much of today's voracious demand is wasteful. The huge appetite towards the use of the earth's precious resources to satisfy the modern lifestyle of the growing population of 7 billion is being questioned. Growth ironically has always been regarded by business leaders as a sustainability strategy.

But increasingly, sustainability advocates question whether such a traditional linear model of produce, consume, and dispose is the right thing to have. Billions of tons of finite resources are being wasted in such a throwaway society. By 2030, the earth's population is expected to hit 10 billion, most of them coming from emerging and less-developed economies.

Greenpeace reported that eight million tonnes of plastic waste have entered the oceans the past five years. Plastic waste is just an example. Across all parts of business and society, there are endless counts of overconsumption, from mobile phones to food. Acknowledging this as a problem is hard, as most regulators would only act when they are convinced that overconsumption is a major contributor to rising price inflation or causes danger to heath and society.

Circular economy

Enter the new concept of circular economy, which the European Commission pioneered and promoted, where resources are utilised based on the 3R concept of *reduce, reuse, and recycle*. The 3R concept is meant to gradually end the existing model of production and consumption, which is unsustainable and not in line with the sustainability principles. Wikipedia defines a circular economy as *an economic system aimed at minimising waste and making the most of resources.*

The assumption towards the reuse of the resources is because of the acceptance that the earth will no longer be able to cope with mountains of trash resulting from consumer-led economies. There are many experts who regard additional pressure on energy use and water consumption to support the production and consumption based on a linear model as simply unsustainable. It is predicted in less than two decades, many parts of the earth will face frequent water shortages, plus the prediction that the earth will get hotter, posing more headaches for policymakers and scientists in their battle with adverse impacts of climate change.

The European Commission is convinced of the alternative model of maximising the utilisation of resources, and the transition to recycling model will not only prolong the lifespan but also reuse the resources with minimal waste.

The concept of circular economy is a noble idea. It attracted positive responses from many international agencies and governments, including the World Economic Forum (WEF), which endorses the concept and, in its own findings, estimates that this potentially is a billion-dollar business that can help create new jobs and sustain the global economies. WEF is confident of the concept of circular economy, where both recycling and reusing are elements of a responsible consumption model, and in line with the UN Sustainable Development Goals. Convinced of such a concept, WEF believes that more concerted efforts be increased towards fresh investments in innovation, invention of technologies necessary to transit to such a circular economy—rightly so. As time goes by, there is a strong belief that by applying the right technologies, especially with the advance of artificial intelligence, the recycling model will help to address today's problems of unwanted waste and prolong the use of resources in a sustainable way.

Achievability and desirability

Despite its positive appeal and the popularity of the 3R concept among politicians and academics, there are equally many that are not convinced, as there are challenges of practicality in both costs and social acceptance of the circular economy that are even harder to put in place.

The question that is being posed is whether a circular economy can be 100 per cent achievable. One of the challenges of a circular economy framework is the practicality of the implementation issues and the achievability of the concept. At the core of such a framework lies the question of waste management, especially at the level where a high percentage of waste is reused and recycled.

The answers are not so straightforward; for example, there are materials that easier to recycle than others. The limits to how much waste of each product can be reused are also matters of concern. There are still gaps in methods being used for testing and evaluation of the impacts. There are also gaps in the understanding and the trade-offs towards reuse and recycling.

Simply put, the recycling process demands components that are required to be broken down. Dismantling is one thing, but reusing is another thing. Certain waste can be chemically hazardous as well as impossible to reuse, while recycling paper will require the right processes as well as the use of energy to carry out the necessary tasks. These challenges and limitations are made known to policymakers, whose recent decision of defining up to 70 per cent recycling remains a massive task.

Investments and capacities

The recycling efforts will require fresh investments plus many fiscal incentives. The reluctance of many private-sector enterprises is because of the uncertainty in financial returns as seen among Asian-based businesses. Coincidentally, these are regions which urgently require sound solid waste management and infrastructures needed for circular economy.

While there is much truth to incentivising businesses to recycle their waste, many who embark on such initiatives are found to be doing it inefficiently; hence, it becomes costly in the long run.

Recycling process is being done through limited capacities, including some places where much of the so-called wastes are exported. Developed economies, for years, have found the easiest route is to export the mountains of wastes to a third-world country for recycling purposes. China was a favourite destination till the government restriction because of environmental hazards and concerns. While some have found their way to South-East Asian markets, there have been actions taken by the governments in Thailand, Malaysia, and the Philippines to return the millions of recycling materials to the original source. Unless the markets start expanding their recycling facilities, the increase in the pile-up of these wastes will continue.

The business case for each of these possibilities is a serious matter; many governments have taken the model of circular economy more seriously, as the process demands the proper facilities, involving production processes that are appropriate and economical. The current framework does not provide proper guidelines towards implementation. Certain know-how is available, but the recycling process is expensive and more worthwhile if there is adequate support and necessary collaboration among the right stakeholders.

Today, there are recycling facilities in most of the urban centres. Access to collection points has been made easier by separation of different materials, from bottles, cans, papers to plastics. In some places, even household washing machines, televisions, and car batteries are being carted away for recycling purposes.

Recycling trend

The startling fact that millions of tons of food go to waste each year that the European Community has an action plan and actions to support the circular economy, and one of the actions includes a revised EU waste legislation adopted on 30 May 2018.

Elsewhere, international agencies and United Nations member states made a commitment to embrace the principles laid out by the UN Sustainable Development Goals. While the aims of the circular economy are to maximise the yields of resources, there are massive changes that incur additional financial costs and inconveniences.

From the consumer perspectives, recycling seems a noble idea, but believing half the world's problem is solved with such a move would be misleading. An outright ban would seem the right thing, but it is not possible under the current circumstances. Challenges are then to raise consumer awareness and cooperation over the use of these plastic materials. Many shoppers, however, may not take notice of these unless warning labelling is imposed, which again is unacceptable from a business standpoint.

Consumer activism can help up to a point; importantly, retailers must do more to push for widespread change in consumer recycling behaviours. Plastic-free retailers have started appearing in Europe but not yet a business mainstream to make a difference.

A top-down effort is a must if sustainability efforts in recycling are to achieve any success. Not everything is easily recyclable. Glass, aluminium, paper, and to some extent, food can be recycled and reused. As recycling becomes more widespread, many of these materials are being reused for something else. This is not an easy process, as recycled materials will require different technology and processes; that's where best practices, price discrimination and incentives, and consumer bodies can come together for single cause.

Challenges

The goal of a circular economy is to maximise the use of the resources that sustain the economy. However, not all the waste collected is recycled or can be recycled. The *Independent* newspaper on 21 January 2019 reported that just 9 per cent of the billions of tonnes of plastic wastes produced by the global community are recycled. At almost every international gathering of business and government leaders, there have been many grand plans and commitments to fight climate change through recycling and reduction of waste. Greenhouse gas emissions have been one of the main adverse consequences of extraction and processing of materials to serve society's needs. The same report from the *Independent* newspaper reminded that much of the 92.8 billion tonnes of minerals, fossil fuels, and metals are consumed to produce the current global goods and services. Natural resources are easily depleted; with new technology, it is now much easier to source and extract to satisfy the throwaway society.

It is hard to imagine a day where a single consumer can last a day without the use of plastic, from the plastic wrapper for storing food in the fridge, to a plastic bottle and sometimes a straw to quench one's thirst, to a plastic bag for shopping purposes. These modern conveniences have raised the standard of living, more so in a throwaway society where speed matters, and disposable, single-use plastic materials have facilitated this convenient process. But all of these may make up the modern lifestyle. The problem is what should society do with the plastic material after the single use? Millions of these plastics turned into waste and ended up in landfills, and worse, in oceans, harming the marine life, and plastic bags that clogged the drains cause flash floods in low-lying areas.

Since the 1950s, a total of eight billion tons of plastic have been produced, and it has got cheaper as time goes by. Plastic does not degrade the same way as paper, and there are limits to the number of times plastic can be recycled. Today, manufacturers are encouraged to use and label the materials used for recycling purposes; all of these involve additional costs. There are now many local governments that have banned single use of plastic straws, cutlery in takeaway food, and even plastic bags. The ban is not outright, as shoppers would be outraged if they are deprived of these conveniences.

Opportunities

Despite these challenges, the circular economy is here to stay, so long as value can be extracted from the waste. McKinsey estimated that economic opportunity from recycling is worth USD55–60 billion. Such an opportunity can be realised once plastic waste is regarded as a resource and not waste. The value chain of such recycling must be accelerated. Much of plastic waste is turned into lower-grade disposable shopping bags, typically regarded as a single use. Further research with government funding should really be prioritised and converted to commercial viability. These will require application of science and technology ensuring and enhancing value of plastic. Investment in innovations will require involvement of relevant stakeholders.

The aims and principles of the circular economy offer lots of hope to accommodate the environmental perspective along with commercial interests, while meeting societal needs. The value creation from the circular economy has the opportunities to move upstream, thereby moving away from single use.

Business opportunities should be made available with government support, and it is within this context that concerns and convenience of the respective stakeholders—retailers, shoppers, and households—be considered to ensure they be allowed to dispose for recycling, and consumer sustainability at an affordable price.

CHAPTER 25

Integrated reporting

Integrated reporting (IR) is a framework for extended corporate reporting where both financial reports and sustainability information are integrated into one report. According to the International Integrated Reporting Council (IIRC), integrated reporting is an evolution of corporate reporting on strategic relevance and conciseness, and future orientation. Integrated reporting brings together a better understanding of the information that is of material importance towards improvement process and risk management, including behaviours, and legal compliance.

According to Ernst & Young, IR is a concept that was created to better articulate a broader set of measures that add or contribute to the long-term value of organisations to society. Central to this philosophy is that value would be shaped and influenced beyond finance, i.e. people, social reputation, environment, community, etc.

Integrated reporting is not a sustainability report. The purpose is to ensure a better understanding of the global and societal issues and how they impact the businesses. An integrated report is not a sustainability report. IR gives a working framework for corporate reporting that has rapidly evolved beyond the sustainability disclosure because of stakeholders' increasing preference and demands for better disclosures of non-financial analytics. Integrated reporting brings together broader perspectives, including both financial and non-financial intelligence in reporting and analytics, giving a more integrated but broader perspective to meet a more diverse demand. Sustainability data should be of the highest quality, and consistency is key. These are non-tangible and lead measures that must be supported by the top management and, importantly, must meet international standards.

Trends

The strategic value of integrated reporting has been well explained and written. The recent KPMG International Survey of Corporate Responsibility Reporting 2017 clearly substantiated this, showing evidence that the integration of both financial and non-financial is being accepted as business reporting mainstream, as more than three fourths of the world's biggest companies now accept and practise such a development in their corporate practice, suggesting information on sustainability issues are more relevant today for their stakeholders.

As the language of sustainability is better understood, the adoption of integrated reporting becomes more relevant and appropriate. Demand for such integrated reporting would come from regulators as standards converge and investors want to know the risk element of their investment portfolios. The unpredictable global economy becomes more unpredictable with the adverse effects of climate change and civil society demanding greater transparency; it is important there would be a balance of their needs against frequent changes taking place in the marketplace.

Positive trends and developments

The increase in the number of companies embracing integrated reporting is seen in Japan, Brazil, Mexico, and Spain, as reported by KPMG. The intent of integrated reporting is to cover all aspects of material importance, from strategy execution to practice of risk management to the triple bottom line impacts involving finance, environment, and society. The interdependence is obvious, as seen in recent trends among the companies that that have embraced transparency at the heart of their disclosure strategy.

The drive towards greater transparency also comes from global convergence of governance standards and responsibility. The investment analysts are demanding data intelligence, which they regard as more than necessary for their investment decisions, as well as to serve the interests of better-informed institutional investors.

Global issues

The tenth edition of KPMG's survey tracks and analyses 4,900 participating companies across forty-nine countries reports on four major emerging sustainability trends:

1. UN SDGs
2. Carbon reduction targets
3. Climate-related financial risks
4. Human rights

A total of 80 per cent of the Global Fortune 250 now reports their corporate sustainability performance, either in the form of stand-alone report or part of their annual reports—a trend that has increased 50 per cent since 2005. There has been a dramatic change in non-financial reporting, which has progressed from purely environmental reporting up until 1999 to sustainability (social, environmental, and economic reporting), which has now become mainstream among Global 250 companies (70 per cent) and is fast becoming so among the top 100 companies (50 per cent).

Industrial sectors with relatively high environmental impact continue to lead in reporting. At global level (G250), more than 80 per cent of the companies are reporting in the electronics, utilities, automotive, and gas sectors. But the most remarkable is the financial sector, which shows more than a twofold increase in corporate responsibility reporting since 2002.

Despite the economic uncertainty and unpredictability, companies that are committed to sustainable business practices have not retreated from their priorities towards disclosures of their environmental and social management performances. It is heartening to note from the KPMG survey and the reports that today's reports contain more substance, more balance, and a wide use of different communications channels to reach their diverse range of stakeholders.

The KPMG survey clearly confirms that reporting on sustainability performance is now part of the business responsibility and obligations—such a development is encouraging, and evidence of improvements as can be seen from a rise in the number of corporate reports that contain information on intangibles.

The use of third-party assurance is positive, although KPMG's survey shows 90 per cent of these come from data verification on carbon emissions. Less than 5 per cent are on social performance. But the survey does indicate that any inclusion of third-party assurance will help towards improvement in quality and reinforce credibility among stakeholders.

Overall, the KPMG survey shows that companies are moving towards a more strategic approach to corporate responsibility management and reporting, and a maturing of the practice seems to be occurring. Top drivers for reporting cited by companies were ethical considerations and innovation—two aspects that will be a key to helping companies steer to success through the challenges in today's prevailing economic climate.

The KPMG survey reflects the growing importance of global issues within the business community of corporate responsibility as the key indicator of non-financial performance, as well as a driver of financial performance. Among the key global issues KPMG's survey reviewed, climate change remains a top business challenge and reporting of greenhouse gas emissions is evidenced in more than 300 global top companies. The improvement in the reports can be seen from the disclosures on the quality of its management, use of quality assurance, to the way sustainability issues are being addressed. KPMG reports show many are disclosing how well they are performing with their climate goals through disclosure of carbon emissions measures, allowing analysts to assess how far corporations have gone with their commitment towards external climate goals such as the Paris Agreement 2°C goal.

The majority of the world's largest companies have now included in their corporate reporting disclosure on their carbon emissions, and among the sample of 100 top companies, 50 per cent are already doing just that. A total of 28 per cent of these companies acknowledge that climate change has already been treated as a financial risk, although very few have gone far enough to analyse and quantify such risks.

A growing trend is the disclosure of a company's stand and position on human rights as an issue for their business. Three quarters of the 100 sample companies are treating human rights as one of top issues in their agenda.

Quality

The quality and relevance of data and analysis in IR is necessary towards better credibility of the reports. It allows a better understanding of the values and leadership styles of management. Such a view is echoed in the survey conducted by ACCA, which showed that of the forty-seven companies that took part, there were significant improvements made in only a year. To begin with, there has been greater consistency, and it is encouraging to note vast improvements in its presentation that shows consistency and good use of benchmarks, data, and industry-wide performance measures. A key differentiation in the framework is that reports should be reliable and complete. This means materiality does matter—both positive and negative should be presented in a balanced way. It is pleasing to see improvements in this area, as it strengthens the credibility of integrated reports. Materiality focuses on matters that affect the risk and opportunity, and these can make a difference to value.

In its annual report 2017, for example, Novartis summarised its mission, vision, and strategy in an admirably clear and concise way, and these underscore the annual report throughout—from the introduction to the report, which quotes the mission, through to variable CEO and executive committee remuneration, which is based on long-term value creation targets. It conveys a very strong sense to report users that innovation is at the heart of Novartis' strategic advantage.

It is good to have companies devoting a detailed analysis of stakeholder engagement across involving issues on talent development, customer health and safety issues, and diversity matters and demonstrating how these are aligned to the company performance.

Another example is UniCredit's 2016 integrated report, which demonstrates an excellent example of how stakeholder engagement takes place regularly in the ordinary course of business. Regular stakeholder engagement has allowed UniCredit to demonstrate an impressively granular understanding of different stakeholder needs, by stakeholder group as well as by country/region.

Assurance

Communication strategies for reporting involve more than just hard reports—online reports or innovative flyers, press advertorials or customer leaflets now provide easy accessibility for the stakeholder to gain relevant information. Product labelling of contents is now more detailed, signifying the emergence of responsible marketing. Most stakeholders will still prefer a printed report or at least updated reports that can be downloaded from the Internet.

Assurance involves incorporating sustainability issues, and it is where companies are expected to talk about business risks, opportunities, and performance regarding, say, climate change or world hunger. Mainstream investors may not request such reports, so the onus is on the companies to alert and highlight these to them.

One of the best European corporate reports is that of Novo Nordisk, a Denmark-based biotech healthcare company, which earned the company the trust capital, and a reputation among its investors, business relations, and employees. The company's 2018 report discusses key challenges and strategic initiatives to sustain long-term value creation and sustainability. The report based on GRI guidelines assures high standards and comparison based on the AA1000 Assurance Standard (2003), Global Reporting Initiative (GRI) G3 Sustainability Reporting Guidelines, and the UN Global Compact Reporting Guidelines. The report's focus on the triple bottom line is externally assured, ensuring that the company is accountable. The company also invites stakeholders' comments on key issues, and the entire process has made the staff proud and has taken sustainability seriously and positively.

Issue-based reporting

Developments of integrated reporting are fast taking shape. It is increasingly common to read companies making their commitment to be part of the global community to address global issues and challenges. It is increasingly necessary for global companies to make their stand, including their position on policy and strategy matters. For example, there are already companies disclosing their carbon footprint and how they intend to address this in their product developments.

The report discloses carbon emissions trends, including their targets, context, clearer communication of issues, and more external verification.

Integrated reporting is about how business manages its long-term value creation by taking an organisation-wide approach involving financial and non-financial perspectives and detailing how these impacts affect the organisation and its stakeholders.

The intent of integrated reporting is to show how the intelligence from the environmental and social responsibilities are being described and measured, and these include the carbon footprint, impacts, and implications of business developments and products on society at large, its stand on human rights, employment conditions, waste management, etc.

So when company embarks on an integrated report, it goes beyond finance, taking broader employee, environmental, and social perspectives and data, to also give a more accurate reading that the business can integrate the broader risks and opportunities into its long-term strategy, into its risk management, into operating policies and procedures, and what the trade-offs are between the issues.

Integrated reporting helps to link the strategic objectives to these critical success factors—an important process of performance management. Hence, it allows the organisation to address risk, external influences, and risks from external environment. In many businesses, integrated reporting will cover the business overview vis-à-vis the issues, the concerned risks and opportunities, its business delivery model, performance management, business planning and outlook.

Future reporting on the issue of climate change will most definitely need a policy statement for companies to set the general principles and framework which they will aim for and to address specific issues relevant to climate change, such as operations, products, and the impact on their stakeholders.

Future trends

Future integrated reports will move towards establishing credibility and measurable reporting. What will make a difference to the readers is when an organisation starts to align its sustainability policy to its evolving business model and the subsequent disclosure on its tangible and measurable impacts on the environment and society will become more mainstream. Integrated reporting is here to stay.

Future reporting will continue to demonstrate the importance of quality management, including managing risks and compliance, increased third-party inputs and stakeholders' inclusiveness in addressing global issues, especially on climate change and human rights.

The framework of integrated reporting will certainly evolve, driven by the need to raise standards of reporting and the need to improve linkages between management of performance and corporate responsibility. All these improvements will certainly reduce the number of glossy reports but improve credibility, improve transparency, and improve stakeholders' trust. One area among integrated reporters is the extent to which new technology is exploited to harness and analyse data and intelligence to enhance their integrated reporting.

As integrated reporting gets better in quality and scope, there will be a need to integrate such reporting into business management processes, where risks, governance, and controls will be better managed. The concept of integrated reporting hence is gaining awareness in the more developed economies.

Companies increasingly are accepting wider accountability, especially to their diverse stakeholders, whose interests can make a difference to the overall reputation, which will have an impact on long-term financial achievements. Accessibility is important, but one thing remains consistent—substance counts more over form.

CHAPTER 26

Artificial intelligence in sustainability

It is hard to imagine the world without technology. From the days of the first industrial revolution of the eighteenth century right up to the current fourth industrial revolution, the role of technology has always been significant and hugely impactful.

Today, technological innovations are developed and applied at much faster rate. As Klaus Schwab speculated in his famous World Economic Forum article (14 January 2016), '*the speed of current breakthroughs has no historical precedent. When compared with previous industrial revolutions, the Fourth is evolving at an exponential rather than a linear pace*'.

Technology has continuously evolved to make our lives much easier, with most of our modern needs and demands conveniently served. For example, the advance of technology through automation has helped industries to be more efficient as well as serving customers better and meeting societal needs. Individuals now have better access to information via the Internet, and this alone has had a major impact on living standards via improved health, education, and safety. The advent of artificial intelligence (AI) promises to further revolutionise our business models as well as the way society operates.

AI technologies have already made a difference to modern living. From online shopping to booking Uber transport or food, the value of such technologies to convenience is very positive. AI has assisted specialists in early detection and causes of illnesses, to even improve safety and health aspects of many organisations.

AI defined

Modern dictionaries today refer to AI as a sub-field of computer science and how machines can imitate human intelligence. The *English Oxford Living Dictionary* defines AI as '*the theory and development of computer systems able to perform tasks normally requiring human intelligence, such as visual perception, speech recognition, decision-making, and translation between languages*'.

AI's contribution to growth and development is not in doubt, but it has brought about considerable changes and further threats to the labour market. A considerable number of traditional jobs have already disappeared as a consequence of an increased employ of computer programs, *algorithms*, or even robots. During this process of structural adjustment with changing job market, many semiskilled and unskilled jobs have disappeared forever.

AI's upside

Despite the inevitable impact on the jobs market, AI offers a significant opportunity to help address the world's sustainability issues. Ensuring sustainability is one of the greatest challenges facing us today and requires concerted efforts in a variety of areas. These include efforts to produce clean energy, food security, healthy lifestyle, green technology, and low-carbon transport, which all require appropriate management of our natural resources.

Managing these will require a strong leadership and conviction. AI needs to be purposefully leveraged to maximise the use of data analytics and data science to address sustainability issues.

In many ways, AI technologies have made much difference to lifestyle of many in modern living. From online shopping to booking Uber transport or food, the value of such technologies to convenience is very positive. The pace of change through AI has made face or voice recognition an identity feature from passports to even issuance of credit cards, and in health care sectors, AI has assisted specialists in early detection and causes of illnesses, to even improve safety and health aspects of many organisations.

AI gaining traction

Elsewhere it's common to come across impacts of AI towards better disclosures through better mining of the narratives and intangibles that companies go about with their CSR activities. Global companies have been quick to make use of AI support analysis of their measures' corporate sustainability reports, for example, to analyse efficiency and emissions reductions, and to innovate new products and services.

The use of AI to forecast weather patterns through its analytics have helped many weather centres to improve forecasts and weather modelling. AI has also assisted utilities companies to better manage their energy load, maximise renewable energy production, and reduce greenhouse gas emissions.

The use of AI in schools, hospitals, and medical facilities means many risks can be managed better in operations where health and safety are critical. Ensuring safer environment, especially in managing the outbreak of contagious disease, has helped with public safety.

These AI applications for sustainability are still at infant stage, but the data analysis suggests there are still untapped benefits for AI to assist in the sustainability challenges.

AI and sustainability

The use of AI to address sustainability changes means no sector should be left behind. Both profit and non-profit institutions can be supported to do their jobs more efficiently, with better intelligence and improved capabilities. At minimum, AI can be used to explore means of reducing energy use or boosting fuel efficiencies.

As AI grows in influence, it is also likely that technology will become more integrated and intrusive to our way of life. Advances in data collection and aggregation, algorithms, and processing power are not likely to dissipate. One will expect AI to continue to be refined for commercial applications. For regulators, AI offers better access and analysis of intelligence to help govern and facilitate enforcement of rules. AI impact on addressing the world's sustainability challenges of environment and society invites further discussion.

AI has offered fresh economic opportunities to all business at large. To an extent, Price Waterhouse Coopers (PWC) reported that AI will contribute economic growth worth $15.7 trillion by 2030. The firm expects the trend of using more AI to continue, even replacing tasks that use human cognition and analysis, including the ability to detect fraud. Already AI is now being deployed in human interventions that are complex and diverse. Switching to the use of AI will change forever the business model across many sustainable businesses, including financial inclusion, green retail, food chains, and even governments.

AI in China

The application of AI is uneven across many markets. China today leads in research and applications of AI. Boston Consulting Group (BCG) in their research found that 85 per cent of Chinese companies are active players in the field of AI, leading all seven nations in the study. BCG identified one explanation for China's dominance, their New Generation Artificial Intelligence Development Plan introduced in 2017, which is delivering strong results. China is expected to become a leading global hub for AI development. The policymakers have recognised that AI is necessary to assist in managing the nation's vast environmental and social challenges. AI would then be able to produce, analyse, and generate huge amounts of intelligence to provide solutions to help the country overcome its infrastructure demands, including building the biggest network of electric trains, renewable energy including solar and hydroelectric. Much of these technologies have boosted productivity and capability for China to sustain its future economic growth as well as contribute to the global battle against climate change. By automating workplaces with AI, the industry could add 0.8 to 1.4 percentage points to GDP growth annually, according to a McKinsey report. By the same token, the McKinsey Global Institute Research suggests that by 2030, that the economic net worth of AI could reach USD13 trillion per year.

AI risks

Today it is harder to imagine a day in the life of anyone without the use of technology, particularly in the developed world. However, the dependence of business and society on technology has become so pervasive that it does bring concerns, risks, and even threats. While technology has supported efficiency outcomes, it has brought challenges, and it invites a reflection on the responsibility and the choices various stakeholders embedded in technology organisations make, and for what purpose.

AI brings choices, benefits, and opportunity costs that can be a double-edged sword. McKinsey Consultants have said that while this could be said of most new technologies, the AI impacts can be more profound and sharper, and only time will tell if the impacts are good or bad.

While AI has by and large contributed much to sustain industry benefits and consumer value, there are risks and unwanted consequences from overreliance on AI. Already because of the huge data, there are fears of privacy invasion and even manipulation of public opinions in political elections. No one will dispute that AI can serve public good, but many sceptics are concerned over its possible social ills. Fake news, manipulation of information are examples where rogue politicians or even international terrorists could use them for self-serving needs. Hurting people is one; there have been instances where AI can be used as a powerful tool to influence the poor for political gains.

Of a greater concern is wrong interpretation of data that leads to disastrous repercussions, including the loss of human life. For example, an AI medical algorithm and interpretation can still go terribly wrong. These are challenges to the organisations, and ensuring AI does their job would be a paramount importance. Many remain cautious over managing possible unintended consequences. Technology and processes are never perfect. They do impact negatively on data integrity and performance of AI. Software failure will not be uncommon, as there will be rare chances that data may not help address the issue concerned.

While technology has helped to drive developments, AI has made it so much easier for industry to exploit and deplete precious resources across land, sea, and forests. Increased intensity can also be bad news for mitigating actions to conserve depleted resources and slow down the effect of pollution.

Ensuring the effectiveness of AI to achieve sustainable development activities will require combined efforts of various stakeholders, especially towards sharing of data responsibly. Accessibility to data plus quality of this intelligence will require the right applications and purpose. AI means automating tasks that require human cognition, such as AI capabilities to augment human decisions on everything from analysis to delivery. AI adoption does come with risks, and unintended consequences can include misuse, abuse, and even sale of data to third parties. These will need to be managed with care.

CHAPTER 27

Humans versus robots

Felicity Healey-Benson

Many global research and analytics firms are conjoined in the view all companies will need to leverage AI techniques to survive the fourth industrial revolution. Yet there are key differences in opinion as to the extent and appeal of the impact.

The positive and pragmatic perspective is that technology has always caused upheaval in job markets. Taking this position, humans should accept the large-scale automation threat to both unskilled and white-collar roles and embrace the new job designs and opportunities that will materialise. The World Economic Forum in 2018 estimated AI and robotics will create a net increase of 58 million jobs by 2022, with PWC claiming these will be focused in health, professional, scientific, technical service, and education roles. The changes are expected to yield improvements for society. For example, the Australian Centre for Robotic Vision reports that intelligent robotics will pave the way for the cost-effective address of global maintenance and construction issues, particularly in dangerous working environments, which include fire, flood, earthquake, and bomb disposal.

In contrast, the dystopian view, epitomised by entrepreneur/futurist Elon Musk, claims an inevitable domination of the robot will undermine the status of humans, threatening their existence. This has unleashed hot debate over the existence and timing of the singularity, as popularised by futurist Raymond Kurzweil, the future moment when software becomes self-aware and smart beyond human capacity to understand. There is concern that the decimation of the labour market will push full responsibility on to governments to make sustenance payments to citizens in lieu of their access to wages.

Whether or not you believe the robots are coming for your job or for humanity, it is difficult to contest that robotics will be a game-changer for most industries, as they integrate into all fields affecting human life.

Human uniqueness

To concurrently evolve alongside the technology, experts on the future of work now fixate on the skills they believe will keep humans productively employed for the foreseeable. Creativity, empathy, and cognitive flexibility are headlined as the ones that will elevate humans above the machines. Let's examine how humans and robots weigh in currently on several predicted future-proofing skills.

Creativity

While AI is clearly most efficient at generating many permutations of options, it is not as good at providing the quality of creative choices humans can achieve. Humans are currently seen as the heavyweights in creativity, with AI at best a tool and space for the expression of human creativity. This position was publicly scrutinised when AI-generated art sold at Christie's in 2018, triggering a global debate as to whether a robot, in fact, could now be an artist. Research into the art piece revealed its production to be based on an AI-human collaboration, crucially employing human intelligence to define the overarching rules and steer the way. In 2016, the IBM Watson cognitive platform was used for the first-ever AI-created movie trailer, for 20th Century Fox's horror movie *Morgan*. Watson analysed the visuals, sound, and composition of hundreds of horror film trailers and then matched them up to scenes from the completed *Morgan* movie, reducing a weeks-long process to one day.

True independent machine creativity cannot be derived from a system based on mathematical functions, yet AI will continue to infiltrate all forms of media and expression. As imagination and dreaming remain unprogrammable skills, entrepreneurs, innovators, artists, and thought leaders will hold advantage over technology. In the future, even the best of the human creatives will make use of smart, efficient, and inspirational robot assistants.

Empathy

Robots learn behaviours from humans through interaction, responding in the most empathetic way found in their data bank. The more interactions and feedback, the more behaviour characteristics gathered so that a robot's empathetic responses to any one person become more refined. This is a form of mimicry. It is not that the robot truly feels, but that it has been programmed to identify and express various feelings picked up from human facial or vocal expressions. Affective computing is the study and development of systems and devices that can recognise, interpret, process, and simulate human affects (feelings/experiences). Over fifty million homes already have an Amazon Echo and Google Home. Robots equipped with numerous sensors built on intelligent assistant technology offer the benefit of emotion recognition feedback during social interactions. It is unlikely roles requiring empathy, such as primary care physicians, caregivers, and therapists will be fully outsourced to robots, but machines will be more intensively employed in these fields in the future.

As robots become more efficient in picking and responding to human signals, humans will need to continue to need to work on their skills. Heavy reliance on technology and the IoT over time can actively stunt emotions and inhibit deep human connection. The trade-off of access to empathetic machines is potentially for humans, a trail of less reciprocal or shallower relationships. As P. J. Manney, humanist/futurist author of *(R) evolution*, explains, empathy works on a neurological system involving a 'theory of mind' network that includes emulation and learning. At the centre of empathy is communication. Despite the unprecedented communication activity facilitated by technology in the modern world, there is still a high level of distrust and conflict. Ideological silos within broadcast, print, websites, and social media have created more extremist views. The sheer volume of information itself, and witness to a barrage of emotionally draining stories can lead to the negation or suppression of emotion that destroys empathy. As Manney warns, twenty-first-century communications technology will both destroy and create empathy, 'but we can actively choose creation. Remember that empathy is a muscle: The more you use it, the stronger it gets'.

Critical thinking

When Russian chess grandmaster Garry Kasparov famously lost to IBM's Deep Blue computer in 1997, the world feared the machines had finally outsmarted human thinking capacity. The win is now attributed to the machine's capacity to perform calculations at a blistering pace. Even two decades of exponential technological advancement later, Kasparov insists AI is a powerful tool not to be feared. Even though a machine can answer a lot of questions very rapidly, humans are still the ones asking the important questions.

AI currently dominates our stock trades and controls the operation of power plants, nuclear reactors, and military nuclear response. Yet no matter how advanced the robots become, it's likely we will still need humans to make key judgements and critical decisions. For example, despite the strides made in AI legal document analysis to date, a human judge is still needed to adjudicate a decision. When machine decisions are inimical to human values, there will always be the propensity to intervene. Humans currently surpass the robot capacity for broad thinking and will rely upon them for relevant advice and data.

Overdependence on data feeds or instant data access and the rise of Google syndrome will not lead to greater knowledge, wisdom, and better decision-making. A dearth of critical thinking of more recent learners and graduates compared to previous generations has triggered a global review of the modern education system, one that has overemphasised memorisation and the regurgitation of facts at the cost of honing the ability to reason, think critically, and problem solve. Without investment in critical thinking, human abilities will atrophy over time. Ironically, it's robotics which may keep humans on their toes and be the tools they need to maintain their critical edge. For example, a robotic enrichment programme combining mathematics, logic, and algorithms can promote computational and critical thinking.

Adaptability and agility

Charles Darwin is reported to have once said that it is not the strongest or most intelligent of the species that survives, but the one most adaptable to change. In a volatile, unpredictable, complex, and ambiguous (VUCA) world, there is indeed heightened pressure on human dynamic strategic behaviours for survival. The global obsession with agility and adaptability exemplifies the importance of embracing unpredictability and change. Humans have a good track record. Anthropological accounts alone reveal the remarkable history of human adaptability and agility. But robot capability should not be underestimated either. AI software can now also write code for itself. Microsoft's Deep Coder can solve its programming problems by stealing codes from other programs. Universities around the world are at work on giving robots a form of situational awareness and promise to make robots truly adaptable. Already, research robots can learn by trial and error and adapt to injuries.

Humans need to keep on top of their game, upping the ante on enhancing processing and learning capabilities. Christof Koch of the Allen Institute for Brain Science in Seattle would argue for the enhancement of cognitive capabilities through direct intervention into the nervous systems. He says only integrating AI chips into neural wiring may address concerns about the rapid rise of AI, and the potential that the machines could outpace humans. Researchers have already found ways to rewire paralysed limbs so that they can respond to brain commands, and even provide sensory feedback. Dr André Vermeulen, founding member and CEO of Neuro-Link, a consultancy specialising in the neuroscience of workplace learning, offers a less invasive route. Vermeulen suggests the human brain is very different from that of the robot, so people should focus on the strategies that will increase their brain fitness to help them excel in their human abilities. They make use of AI instead as the accelerator to what they want or can achieve.

Aptitude for learning

Born from pattern recognition, machine learning (ML) is a technique that lets a robot 'learn' how to better perform on a specific task without being explicitly programmed, making decisions with minimal human intervention. The highly complex nature of real-world problems, though, often means the ability of specialised algorithms to solve them correctly every time is impractical. To date, machines are still incapable of mimicking the way children learn autonomously by forming original hypotheses. Humans should be focused now on building their capacity through agile learning to optimise the drivers that influence their brain performance. Humans today, even older generations, have embraced and adapted to a breadth of technological offerings, from the way they socialise, communicate, work, shop, and learn. For example, Ofcom in the UK revealed record numbers of older people embrace smart and social technology, with a quarter of over-75s using tablet computers. Humans continue to prove they are natural-born learners.

Sustainability

On numbers alone, as humankind moves towards eight billion, the Global Footprint Network estimates humans deplete their annual supply of renewable resources by August every year, at which point the non-renewable supplies are used. This is stealing from future generations. Conservationists warn robots, incredibly energy-hungry and difficult to recycle, will further accelerate unsustainable, insupportable damage to the planet. The worldwide insatiable demand for e-products will continue to place unsustainable demands on raw materials, particularly the nickel, cobalt, and graphite used in lithium-ion battery production. The environmental damage includes the toxic chemicals which leak from the evaporation pools into the water supply, soil degradation, and air contamination. Continuing to enhance the computing power of robots will exacerbate matters, as they are likely to require much more energy use in the future.

While robots have enabled progress for science, production efficiencies, and quality of life, including the release of labour from the more dangerous and dirty jobs, robot insides are mostly toxic. They are made of non-biodegradable plastic or metallic substances. Biodegradable robotic organisms and smart materials already in development may make some dent in this.

Avoid harm

It would be improper to not draw account to the actual potential for robots to house a dangerous superintelligence. Robots have caused harm. In Germany, a worker at a Volkswagen plant was crushed to death by a robot that apparently mistook him for a car part, errors that wouldn't have been made by a human observer. There is also the worry that robots in the wrong hands could lead to devastating consequences. Oxford philosopher Nick Bostrom suggests 'we're like small children playing with a bomb'. Adversarial data describes a situation in which human users intentionally supply an algorithm with corrupted information. The corrupted data throws off the ML process, tricking the algorithm into reaching fake conclusions or incorrect predictions.

There is also a growing fear that global power lies with an elite that own the enterprises we all send our data to, and AI consolidates their power further. Yuval Noah Harar, author of *Homo Deus: A Brief History of Tomorrow* claims 'democracy and the free market will both collapse once Google and Facebook know us better than we know ourselves'—that authority will shift from individual humans to networked algorithms. Conspiracy of the ruling elite aside, there are real issues to deconstruct, between whether mass data sharing fuels democracy and equality, or is employed as an authoritarian tool that monitors and controls. To this end, a future-fit education must protect humans by embracing technology but also ensure learners with the right skills thrive and think for themselves.

Complacency

Overall, the evidence suggests humans are not likely to be displaced by robots in the immediate future. Yet the human condition itself and all its fallibilities will undermine their relative strength. Across the globe, humans struggle with complex issues and world order. At present, the masses, particularly in the developed countries, are addicted to their devices, making use of algorithm-parsed data to navigate their lives. Online addiction behaviours and mental health issues are growing exponentially among the youth. Technology simplifies and enhances our lives, but it is also a form of dependency and a source of distress and control. The human technological appetite and the resources machines deplete in their production and use potentially outweigh their efficiencies. At the same time, there is a global leadership crisis. While robots of the future will not all be humanoid, in short, robots will become ubiquitous.

Rather than dwell on fear, humans should prepare to take advantage of their assistance and augmentation. History has shown humans push past boundaries, with a strong instinct to explore and create, yet these very instincts will dwindle if not actively cultivated. Given the skills will be crucial in the future workplace and society, it is imperative they are instilled through the education system of the present. Humans are not born with developed skills; they need to be grown and continuously enhanced. It is also important that humans take the lead on the ethics that will ultimately shape the redesign of further advanced technological society.

Humans versus robots is not a zero-sum game. With the help of machines, humans can achieve intelligent automation, achieving enhanced role specialisation, improved decision-making and increased productivity, innovation, and efficiency. Humans are the creators, not the robots, but humans need to mindful of who is controlling the code.

CHAPTER 28

Future of sustainability

The *Guardian* newspaper on 26 July 2019 carried a headline that read *'All-time temperature records tumble again as heatwave sears Europe'*. Such headlines are increasingly common in this day and age. Hot summers, forest fires, prolonged droughts, and unexpected floods are evidence of disruptive weather patterns.

Shifting weather patterns are not our only sustainability challenge; food security, waste and water pollution, diminishing forest resources, and housing shortages abound against the background of rising population in an uncertain environment. Ecological and social challenges are real.

A linear approach to a more sustainable world can no longer continue. Different perspectives have been sought. The consensus is that more needs to be done beyond rhetoric and words.

Sustainability directions

For many, a common question posed is what the future holds for sustainability. The United Nations SDGs, adopted by all member countries in 2015, provide a welcome clarity and direction for world leaders and communities on what needs to be done to deliver a more sustainable future for all.

The set of seventeen goals are intended to address a broad set of global concerns and challenges including poverty, access to education, social inequality including gender discrimination, climate change, and worsening environmental degradation.

Ecological and social challenges

Today, politicians, businesses, and consumers recognise sustainability challenges are here to stay and are now just awakening to the fact today's convenience may be sacrificing a sustainable future. The obvious evidence on the unintended consequences from the burning of fossil fuel, high carbon footprints, billions of tons of waste, and the fast disappearance of our forest resources from the land and fish from the ocean have now heightened levels of concerns.

The prevailing environmental and social issues translate into complex challenges for policymakers. An example is plastic waste pollution which remains unresolved despite the awareness and actions taken. The BBC reporting on plastic particles falling out of sky into snow in the Arctic on 14 August 2019 highlights the extent of the crises.

Decades after plastic first appeared as very adaptable polymer in the 1950s, the contented society has become highly dependent on the convenience and adaptability of its uses. Overcoming this dependency continues to be a challenge. Plastic is cheap and easy to use, yet minimal attention is given to the environmental consequence of its production and disposal. Despite the growing ban on the single-use bag, which has encouraged shopper environmental attitudes, this is an insignificant dent when the National Geographic reports that plastic production is forecast to double by 2040 from 2019.

Recycling plastic in a new circular economy holds many promises, but it is too early to say whether it offers a permanent solution to the adverse effects of the billions of tons of plastic waste the world has produced.

Climate change

Despite the denials that climate change has nothing to do with the many abnormal weather patterns, there is a consensus among leading stakeholders, including political and corporate leaders, that there is real urgency to address the climate agenda and that commitment to the sustainable development goals is the right thing to do.

At the United Nations Climate Change Conference, and the 24th Conference of the Parties to the United Nations Framework Convention on Climate Change in Katowice, Poland, December 2018, the famous and highly respected British naturalist Sir David Attenborough said, '*Right now we are facing a man-made disaster of global scale, our greatest threat in thousands of years: climate change. If we don't take action, the collapse of our civilisations and the extinction of much of the natural world is on the horizon*'.

One significant outcome of the conference was the agreement among the signatories to accept the rulebook on how to roll out and apply the Paris Climate Accord agreement. While there were no perfect solutions to resolve the global challenge of limiting global temperature rise to 1.5°C above pre-industrial levels and reaching net-zero emissions by no later than 2050, the conference agreed on implementation rules, measures, and reporting. More countries have since committed themselves to more ambitious climate targets aligned with the conference targets.

The International Climate Agreement has endorsed the urgent need to scale up the global response because developments so far towards carbon-emission reduction are less than satisfactory. The consumption of fossil fuel hasn't come down fast enough. Although it is a positive move that more governments have set ambitious plans to go green, renewable energy requires substantial investment.

Even with global actions to help control a rise in global temperature within the 1.5°C range, there is high risk of the global community falling short of this goal. Britain's Prince Charles and the Potsdam Climate Institute founder Hans Joachim Schellnhuber highlighted this situation as a crisis. Even such harsh language commonly used to describe the changing state of the climate doesn't sufficiently convey the enormity of the crisis. The Intergovernmental Panel on Climate Change (IPCC) has announced that the carbon emission needs to be reduced by 45 per cent by 2030 in order to keep global temperatures from rising more than 1.5°C above pre-industrial levels.

The editorial comment in the *Economist* newspaper of 27 July 2019 reaffirms that heat is one of climate change's deadliest manifestations. The leading newspaper reports 30,000 lives were lost during a 2003 heat wave in Europe. A point noted here is that is that the hardest hit by heat waves are those who can least afford not to adapt. In poorer countries where communities are packed into small dwellings with only tin roofs over their heads, such conditions are deadly. More needs to be done to protect the populations in both rich and poor countries from the effect of climate change.

Business sustainability agenda

In response to environmental challenges, twenty-eight multinationals from the business community, with a capital size of USD1.3 trillion, are committed to new climate targets in response to the climate goals, by no later than 2050. There are others which have long repositioned their climate strategy as part of their commitment to embrace the UN Sustainable Development Goals. One example is CERES, a sustainability non-profit coalition of companies devoted to sustainability leadership in its efforts to influence investors and overcome challenges of climate change, water scarcity, pollution, and workplace inclusion.

The need for higher efficiency, less waste means being greener in design and feel is a must. While recycling has become a popular trend that reflects well upon the image of good business, there is a long road ahead to achieve carbon-neutral economies. To begin with, practical solutions for switching to a cleaner, low-carbon economy will require investment.

Actions on harnessing the potential of technological innovation will continue to take place. Much of these are related to infrastructure, from installing wind turbines to more energy-efficient transport systems and changing policies and rules, all cost money.

A higher percentage of these will be led through public sector interventions. There are also challenges of accessibility and affordability, given that funding is not necessarily available quite easily, as well as the concerns of governance and corruption that impede progress and development.

China and sustainable future

Government leadership is essential to drive the required change. From education to enforcement, fiscal measures will make the difference. China, as one of the world's polluters and producers of greenhouse gases, is fully committed to improving its environment and social infrastructures. Its leadership is fully aware of the need to harmonise the environment and innovations and has invested in key initiatives.

China is committed to meeting its SDGs; it has a long-term road map that is well placed to build a more sustainable future. China has made it more difficult and costly to pollute the air and water. It is the country's leadership that has supported efforts to harness the right technology with support from its enterprises, and through its policies.

The World Economic Forum reports that China's war on pollution has produced tangible changes. Initiatives include

1. plans towards the replacement of coal-fired power plants
2. improved regulations, especially on quality of water
3. a greener economy.

In 2014, the country invested USD40 billion in the world's biggest solar farm. Bloomberg reported that of the 385,000 electric buses in the world in 2017, 99 per cent were in China. China has also built the biggest network of high-speed rail, a massive shift from the slow, dirty coal-fired trains.

For its long-term policy, the country's leadership has produced a new whitepaper, *Technology and China's Green Development—Innovating an Environmentally Sustainable Future*. This provides a road map for companies in China and around the world to use technology for sustainability, from compliance and mitigating risk to improved efficiencies, with the potential to transform business for responsible growth. China has been able to demonstrate to the rest of the world the achievability of changing its high greenhouse gas emission position. It's now one of the more sustainable nations despite its 1.5 billion people. The state-owned enterprises, with cooperation of the private sector, are leveraging on utilising technology to build their greener, sustainable future. China may be the exception in its commitment to move in the right directions to shape the future of sustainability.

Question of affordability

The transition to a greener economy or even a low-carbon economy is costly in both financing and educating consumer buy-in. The use of clean technology is costly and may not be as affordable, when compared to the more traditional energy sources such as firewood, coal, or fossil fuel. Besides, not all countries have access to natural resources that enable the harnessing of wind or water power. There are technologies that may not be market ready or affordable or well adapted to end-user needs.

Fresh capital investment would also be required if the circular economy is to become more mainstream and successful. The design of recycling waste is going to take more work, and it takes time for the technology to be made affordable so that products and materials continue to be usable, safe, and cost-effective; the circular economy also has the challenge to regenerate and renew old systems.

Consumerism

The rise in consumerism has led to a throwaway society. Successive economic growth since the 1990s has resulted in a sharp hike in consumption, from tourism to mobile phone communications. Consumer demand has fuelled profit-orientated company success. Greenpeace, for example, believed Coca-Cola was selling almost 128 billion plastic bottles of Coke in 2017, and global sugar consumption reached an all-time high of 170 million metric tons. Rise in consumption means rising extraction of resources, adding more stress on the fragile ecosystem. There are obvious consequences of rising consumerism. Civil society has already highlighted that rising consumerism has led to uncontrolled depletion of earth's resources.

Changing consumer behaviours will be a challenge, but over time, more responsible consumers through product labelling will also influence suppliers within the global chain and put further pressure on governments and business to employ technologies that will drive greater environmental efficiency or products that inflict less damage. Consumers demanding products and services will be a key driver of the innovations that are needed. Yet consumers themselves need to be educated on their shared responsibility. Companies will not produce if it is not demanded.

Innovation

Innovations can be further incentivised through effective fiscal measures and recognition through governance mechanisms at the national level. At the industry level there are opportunities to embrace responsible sourcing throughout the supply chains. Incentives to recognise these efforts should not be ignored.

While such efforts while may not answer or resolve the global sustainability concerns, the bigger nations need to escalate the global agenda including the sharing of systems and technologies for sustainable development. An equitable distribution impacting on energy systems, waste management, food security, education, and water resources are all immediate concerns that will need to be addressed for the future of sustainability. Realising the potential of technology will probably provide one answer to overcome the hard challenges of meeting the sustainable development goals.

Urgency

Applying sustainability requires both political will and investment. One study from Brookings Institute as of 2015, says that governments around the world have spent almost USD21 trillion on sustainable-development-related initiatives involving heath, education, agriculture, infrastructures, justice, and conservation. The trend is likely to go upwards, and the challenge is sustaining funding. Predictably, the more advanced markets have spent more, widening the gap between rich and poor nations. One implication is that the more advanced economies will be better prepared in their mitigating measures, given the assumption that they can afford to spend more.

The future of sustainability initiatives cannot be dependent on one single thing or a 'one size fits all' policy or simply deployment of new technology. It depends on how these three elements come together to produce the outcomes for the good of the earth as a whole. Governments and business leaders today must be prepared to recognise the responsibility that each of the stakeholders have to continue to serve the communities, cities, and world better.

Such fragility is echoed in a new report *The Future is Now: Science for Achieving Sustainable Development*. The report contains inputs from an independent group of scientists and

United Nations appointed experts highlighting the urgency in embracing change towards relationship between people and nature. Emphasising that the immeasurable amount of prosperity, development and progress from both extraction and consumption of resources, the report warns the risk of growing inequality and negative effects of uncontrollable consumption that will derail the achievement of sustainable development goals. The experts in the report acknowledged the challenge in bringing about attitudinal change but in their word they recognised *deep scientific understanding is needed to anticipate and mitigate the tensions and trade-offs inherent in widespread structural change.*

The fragile world needs to evolve in ways that redefine and reshape how business, people and society connect to each other. The use of technology is one example. The digital revolution is changing the way intelligence is being deployed and applied to aid economic and social advancements. These developments generate innovation for developmental purposes. However, these developments will bring about unwanted social repercussions such as possible loss of jobs, worsening income inequality, and even intrusion into privacy of individuals.

All of these changes are painful at times, and one may even encounter resistance from society that is comfortable with the conveniences. Although awareness of the sustainability concerns is rising, there is a broad agreement among sustainability advocates that beyond applications of adaptation and mitigation actions sustainability will evolve to the next level. This will come with the right common attitudes towards environments and better use of resources to ensure universal community developments and food security and deployment of science and responsibility to safeguard the fragile eco system.

ABOUT THE AUTHORS

Tay Kay Luan is the vice chancellor of the International University Malaya Wales and author of *Perspectives on Social and Business Sustainability*. He graduated from the London School of Economics and Political Science, and Kingston University London.

Felicity Healey-Benson, founder of EmergentThinkers.com is a HR/Leadership Lecturer and doctoral candidate at the University of Wales Trinity St. David. Her research focuses on future-proofing educator professional development. She graduated from the London School of Economics and Political Science and Swansea University.

CPSIA information can be obtained
at www.ICGtesting.com
Printed in the USA
LVHW040102091121
702830LV00010B/1083

9 781543 754407